SPORTS in AMERICA
1900–1919

JAMES BUCKLEY, JR.
AND JOHN WALTERS

SERIES FOREWORD BY LARRY KEITH

Facts On File, Inc.

1900–1919
Sports in America

Copyright © 2004 James Buckley Jr. and John Walters
Foreword copyright © 2004 Larry Keith

Facts On File, Inc.
132 West 31st Street
New York NY 10001

Library of Congress Cataloging-in-Publication Data

Sports in America / produced by the Shoreline Publishing Group.
   v. cm.
Includes bibliographical references and indexes.
Contents: [1] 1910-1919 / by James Buckley, Jr. and John Walters — [2] 1920-1939 / by John Walters — [3] 1940-1949 / by Phil Barber — [4] 1950-1959 / by Jim Gigliotti — [5] 1960-1969 / by David Fischer — [6] 1970-1979 / by Timothy J. Seeberg and Jim Gigliotti — [7] 1980-1989 / by Michael Teitelbaum — [8] 1990-2003 / by Bob Woods.

ISBN 0-8160-5233-6 (hc : set : alk. paper) — ISBN 0-8160-5234-4 (hc : v. 1 : alk. paper) — ISBN 0-8160-5235-2 (hc : v. 2 : alk. paper) — ISBN 0-8160-5236-0 (hc : v. 3 : alk. paper) — ISBN 0-8160-5237-9 (hc : v. 4 : alk. paper) — ISBN 0-8160-5238-7 (hc : v. 5 : alk. paper) — ISBN 0-8160-5239-5 (hc : v. 6 : alk. paper) — ISBN 0-8160-5240-9 (hc : v. 7 :alk. paper) — ISBN 0-8160-5241-7 (hc : v. 8 : alk. paper)

1. Sports—United States—History.   I. Buckley, James, 1963-   . II. Shoreline Publishing Group. III. Facts on File, Inc.

GV583.S6826 2004
796'.0973'0904—dc22

                                                                    2004004276

Produced by the Shoreline Publishing Group LLC
President/Editorial Director: James Buckley Jr.
Contributing Editors: Jim Gigliotti, Beth Adelman
Text design by Thomas Carling, Carling Design, Inc.
Cover design by Pehrsson Design and Cathy Rincon
Index by Nanette Cardon, IRIS

Photo credits: Page 1: Courtesy Sports Immortals, Inc. This collection of gear is from the career of one of America's greatest all-around athletes, Jim Thorpe (pages 67 and 70), who won Olympic gold medals and excelled in college and pro football. A member of the Sac and Fox Native American nation, his heritage is represented in the photo by his own handmade beaded gloves.
Interior photos: AP/Wide World: 15, 19, 23, 38, 62, 65, 70, 72, 75, 76, 80, 87, 104; Corbis: 11, 30, 37, 55, 56, 58, 61, 66, 69, 79, 82, 83, 84, 89, 91, 93, 95, 97, 98, 100-101; Baseball Hall of Fame: 25, 26, 35, 46, 48; Hulton Archive: 45; Indiana State Museum: 17; ISC Archives: 27; Transcendental Graphics: 7, 9, 43, 53, 103.
Sports icons by Bob Eckstein.

Printed in the United States of America.

VH PKG 10 9 8 7 6 5 4 3 2 1

This book is printed on acid-free paper.

CONTENTS

Walter Johnson of the Washington Senators (page 74)

FOREWORD

BY LARRY KEITH

IN THE FALL OF 1984, STUDENTS AT COLUMBIA University's prestigious Graduate School of Journalism requested that a new course be added to the curriculum—sports journalism.

Sports journalism? In the graduate program of an Ivy League institution? Get serious.

But the students were serious, and, as students will do, they persisted. Eventually, the school formed a committee to interview candidates for the position of "adjunct professor." As it happened, though, the committee wasn't just looking for a professional sports journalist to teach the course part time. That august body wanted to hear clear and convincing arguments that the course should be offered at all.

In other words, did sports matter? And, more to the point, should an institution that administered the Pulitzer Prize, the highest award in journalism, associate itself with the coverage of "fun and games?"

Two decades later, I am pleased to say that Columbia did decide to offer the course and that it remains in the curriculum. With modest pride, I confess that I helped make the arguments that swayed the committee and became the new adjunct professor.

I reflected on that experience when the *Sports in America* editors invited me to write the Foreword to this important series. I said then, and I say now, "Sport is an integral part of American society and requires the attention of a competent and vigilant press." For our purposes here, I might also add, "because it offers insights to our history and culture."

Sports in America is much more than a compilation of names, dates, and facts. Each volume chronicles accomplishments, advances, and expansions of the possible. Not just in the physical ability to run faster, jump higher, or hit a ball farther, but in the cognitive ability to create goals and analyze how to achieve them. In this way, sports, the sweaty offspring of recreation and competition, resemble any other field of endeavor. I certainly wouldn't equate the race for a gold medal with the race to the moon, but the essentials are the same: the application of talent, determination, research, practice, and hard work to a meaningful objective.

Sports matter because they represent the best and worst of us. They give us flesh-and-blood examples of courage and skill. They often embody a heroic human interest story, about overcoming poverty, injustice, injury, or disease. The phrase, "Sports is a microcosm of life," could also be, "Life is a microcosm of sports." Consider racial issues, for example. When Jackie Robinson of the Brooklyn Dodgers broke through Major League Baseball's color barrier in 1947, the significance extended beyond the national pastime. Precisely because baseball *was* the national pastime, this important event reverberated throughout American society.

To be sure, black stars from individual sports had preceded him (notably Joe Louis in boxing and Jesse Owens in track and field), and others would follow (Arthur Ashe in tennis and Tiger Woods in golf), but Robinson stood out as an important member of a *team*. He wasn't just playing with the Dodgers, he was traveling with them, dressing with them, eating with them, living with them. The benefits of integration, the recognition of its humanity, could be appreciated far beyond the borough of Brooklyn.

Sports have always been a laboratory for social issues. Robinson integrated big-league box scores eight years before the U.S. Supreme Court ordered the integration of public schools. Women's official debut in the Olympic Games, though limited to swimming, came in 1912, seven years before they got the right to vote. So even if these sports were late in opening their doors, in another way they were ahead of their time. And if it was necessary to break down some of those doors—Title IX support since 1972 for female college athletics comes to mind—so be it.

Another area of social importance, particularly as it affects young people, is substance abuse. High school, college, and professional teams are united in their opposition to the illegal use of drugs, tobacco, and alcohol. In most venues, testing is mandatory and tolerance is zero. Perhaps the most celebrated case occurred at the 1988 Olympic Games, when Canada's Ben Johnson surrendered his 100-meter gold medal after failing a drug test. Some athletes have lost their careers, and even their lives, to substance abuse. Other athletes have used their fame and success to caution young people about submitting to peer pressure and making poor choices.

Fans care about sports and sports personalities because they provide entertainment and identity. But they aren't the only ones who root, root, root for the home team. Government bodies come on board because sports spur local economies. When a city council votes to help underwrite the cost of a stadium or give financial advantages to the owners of a team, it affects the pocketbook of every taxpayer, not to mention the local ecosystem. When high schools and colleges allocate significant resources to athletics, administrators believe they are serving the greater good, but at what cost? These decisions are relevant far beyond the sports page.

In World War II, America's sporting passion inspired President Franklin Roosevelt to say professional games should not be cancelled. He felt the benefits to the national psyche outweighed the security risk of gathering huge crowds at central locations. In 2001, another generation of fans also continued to attend large-scale sports events because to do otherwise would "let the terrorists win." Being there, yelling your lungs out, cheering victory and bemoaning defeat, is a cleansing, even therapeutic exercise. The security check at the gate is just another price of stepping inside.

Unfortunately, there's a downside to all this. The notion that "Sports build character" is better expressed "Sports *reveal* character." We've witnessed too many coaches and athletes break the rules of fair play and good conduct, on and off the field. We've even seen violence and cheating in youth sports, often by parents of a (supposed) future superstar. We've watched fans "celebrate" championships with destructive behavior. I would argue, however, that these flaws are the exception, not the rule, that the good of sports outweighs the bad, that many of life's success stories took root on an athletic field.

Any serious examination of sports leads, inevitably, to the question of athletes as role models. Pro basketball star Charles Barkley created quite a stir in 1993 when he declared in a Nike shoe commercial, "I am not paid to be a role model." The knee-jerk response was, "But kids look up to you!" Barkley was right to raise the issue, though. He was saying that, in making lifestyle choices in language, clothing, and behavior, young people should look elsewhere for role models—ideally in their own home, to responsible parents.

The fact remains, however, that athletes occupy an exalted place in our society, at least when they are magnified in the mass media, and especially in the big-business, money-motivated sports. The athletes we venerate can be as young as a high school basketball player or as old as a Hall of Famer. (They can even be dead, as Babe Ruth's commercial longevity attests.) They are honored and coddled in a way few mortals are. We are quick—too quick—to excuse their excesses and ignore their indulgences. They influence the way we live (the food on our table, the cars in our driveway) and think (Ted Williams inspired patriotism as a fighter pilot during World War II and the Korean conflict; Muhammad Ali's opposition to the Vietnam War on religious grounds, validated by the Supreme Court, inspired the peace movement). No wonder we elect them—track stars, football coaches, baseball pitchers—to represent us in government. Meanwhile, television networks pay exorbitant sums to sports leagues so their teams can pay fortunes for players' services.

It has always been this way. If we, as a nation, love sports, then we, quite naturally, will love the men and women who play them best. In return, they give us entertainment, release, and inspiration. From the beginning of the 20th century until now, *Sports in America* is their story—and ours.

Larry Keith is a former writer and editor at Sports Illustrated. *He covered baseball and college basketball and edited the official Olympic programs in 1996, 2000 and 2002. He is a former adjunct professor of sports journalism at Columbia University and is a member of the Board of Visitors of the University of North Carolina School of Journalism.*

INTRODUCTION
1900–1919

Sports in America as the 20th century opened was a very different animal than it is today. No National Football League. No National Basketball Association. One league in Major League Baseball. No Rose Bowl. No NASCAR. No Indy 500. No professional tennis or golf. The Olympics were only four years old. There was no radio, no TV, no cable, no ESPN, no Internet, and no color photography. Fans knew their sports heroes only through the written word or rare personal viewings.

But things were changing. America was becoming a very different place than it had been for its first 150 years or so. Thanks to the Industrial Revolution and the rise of large populations, creating urban cultures in major cities, more and more people not only had a little extra time on their hands (because you needed time to follow sports), they had a little extra money to spend on such diversions. What had been a largely rural nation was becoming a nation of city-dwellers. A middle class was growing, and working six days a week, 12 hours a day was becoming less and less the norm. Into that empty space of leisure time stepped sports.

Wrote Richard D. Mandell in *Sports: A Cultural History*, "The integration of sport in the working classes was aided by better and cheaper transportation [notably street cars in cities] and communication, greater disposable income, shorter working hours, and the assimilation of second generation children."

That second generation of children looked to sports as one important way to define themselves as Americans. An immigrant child might have trouble climbing the ladder of business success, but with talent and hard work, a life could be made in sports. Baseball, in particular, was populated by many second- and third-generation Irish and German Americans.

The first decade of the 20th century saw the rise of several popular sports. The sports themselves had already been invented by then (for the most part)—baseball had been around more than 50 years, for instance, and the first college football game was played in 1869—but they became much more popular as events for people to watch. This was the era of the spread of spectator sports.

Baseball led the way in this, as it had since becoming the National Pastime in the years after the Civil War. No other sport was as well-organized on a national level (as national as sports got—there

The Growing Crowd *For the first time, there were many sports to watch and many people to watch them.*

were no Major League Baseball teams west of St. Louis), and no other sport was as pervasive throughout American culture. With the birth of the second major league, the American League, in 1901, baseball began a rapid ascent to the top of the American pro sports scene—a spot it would enjoy for another 75 years or so. In the 15 years following 1901, numerous new stadiums were built, using the latest in steel construction techniques, all in an effort to build greater, larger, and better venues to attract paying customers. The World Series was born in 1903 and galvanized national attention on baseball's first annual championship.

People certainly gathered to watch sports in earlier years (the first ballpark that charged admission opened in 1871 in Brooklyn, New York, and horse racing had been a popular diversion in America since colonial days), but in this new century and new national mindset, the idea of watching people who were paid to play sports began to take firmer hold.

The *Saturday Evening Post*, as close as America had in those days to a national newspaper, reflected this belief about the coming rise of sports with these words, published in 1901:

> The American love of sports has risen to a pitch never before known. Until the middle of the century just closed we were practically without sports, and even until some fifteen years ago there was very little enthusiasm aroused by sports compared with the fever that has within the

1900–1919

past decade and a half swept over the country.

Year by year the ardent fervor has been increasing, and the coming season promises to be the most enthusiastic of all.

Baseball wasn't alone, of course, in attracting fans. In some corners of the nation, college football outstripped baseball in popularity. But the sport also nearly disappeared, almost done in by its own inherent violence. In the years before World

Native Son *The son of German immigrants, baseball star Honus Wagner represented a growing trend in sports.*

War I, college football's near-demise and rapid rebirth proved to be an important part of the sports story of the day.

Baseball and football was about it for team sports. Whereas today the four major team sports dominate headlines for both pro and college spectator sports, early in the 20th century, fans looking for their sports fix turned to many individual sports, notably boxing, horseracing, and bicycle racing. In a telling note of the coming "modern" world, bicycle racing was eclipsed almost overnight by automobile racing.

In boxing, an important strand of the American sports story was beginning to be told. With a few exceptions (see Major Taylor, page 16), African Americans were not welcome in this new, wider world of sports. Baseball unofficially banned all black players, while golf and tennis clubs were, as the saying goes, as white as the balls they used. In boxing, however, several African-American athletes reached the pinnacle of the sport, most notably Jack Johnson, one of the key figures of the era. Johnson's stunning skills and equally powerful personality presaged in many ways the cult of athletic celebrity that came to full flower nearly 100 years later. But at the time, Johnson fought not only his opponents, but a public that was growing less interested in watching black athletes compete. They rooted openly for him to lose to white boxers. Remember, this was about 40 years before Jackie Robinson's historic start with the Brooklyn Dodgers baseball team.

While more and more people flocked to watch sports, huge numbers also began to participate in one way or another. Again, the idea that hard-working people had some time off was a new one, and a wave of experts promoted the values of sport in a healthy life—whether sandlot baseball, pick-up football, tennis, running races, or "calisthenics" (the 1900 version of aerobics). It's important to note that women were using this flowering of sport to gain a foothold in athletics of all sorts. While they were decades away from the breadth of participation enjoyed today, it became more and more prevalent for women to do some sort of sporting activity.

Sports, like America itself, was growing and growing. This book documents the early stages of that growth, focusing on the rise of spectator sports, while touching on some of the important milestones in participation sports, too.

As the *Saturday Evening Post* concluded in 1901:

Ahead of His Time *Setting the stage for so many to follow, boxer Jack Johnson was perhaps the first truly international sports superstar who was also African American.*

This is the era of sport. Practically every man and boy, woman and girl, takes part or wishes to take part in some branch of it. And it is fortunate that the field is broad enough for all.

In all this eager devotion to it, there is nothing harmful, nothing that points a warning. On the contrary, it is for individual and national good. It gives health and tone to the system, it clears and freshens the mind by bright exercise and competition in the clear, open air, and it drives cobwebs from wearied brains. And thus it is that this era of enthusiastic devotion to sport is good.

In these years, for the first time, sports began to "matter." No ESPN? No problem.

1900

An Underwhelming Olympic Games

The ancient Greeks had created the multi-sport, multi-nation Olympic Games more than 2,500 years ago, and in 1896, under the direction of Frenchman Baron Pierre de Coubertin (1863–1937), they were revived. In tribute to the ancient Greeks, the first modern Games were held in Athens. The aim was not only to create an international competition, but also to re-create the ancient Greek Olympic ideals of brotherhood, peace, and respect among nations. The Athens Games were a resounding success, and the world looked forward to more Olympics.

Unfortunately, four years later, the second modern Olympics were filled with anything but goodwill. A combination of personal crises (including the death of his young son) and political struggles (powerful forces combined to force the Games to go to Paris in 1900) led to the exclusion of de Coubertin—and the International Olympic Committee that he had founded—from planning the Games. The competition went on from May 20 to October 28, but in a far different form than its modern inventor had envisioned.

There were no opening ceremonies, for example, and the name "Olympic Games" was not even used. Organizers and contemporary press reports offered up a variety of substitutes, including "International Championships," "Paris Championships," and "Concours internationaux d'exercises physiques et de sport" (international competition of exercise and sport). The government of France did not adequately support the Games, mixing them in with an already-planned international exposition, and attendance suffered.

While Olympics fans today would recognize the swimming, fencing, yachting, gymnastics, and equestrian events, the 1900 Games also offered ballooning, fireman's drill, auto racing, tug-of-war, cricket, live pigeon shooting, and the always-interesting 200-meter swim through an obstacle course.

American athletes dominated the track-and-field events. Ray Ewry, in particular, was outstanding, although he had suffered from polio (a degenerative muscle and nerve disease) as a child. He won the standing long jump, the standing high jump, and the standing hop, step, and jump (today's triple jump). Alvin Kranzlein began what would become nearly a century of

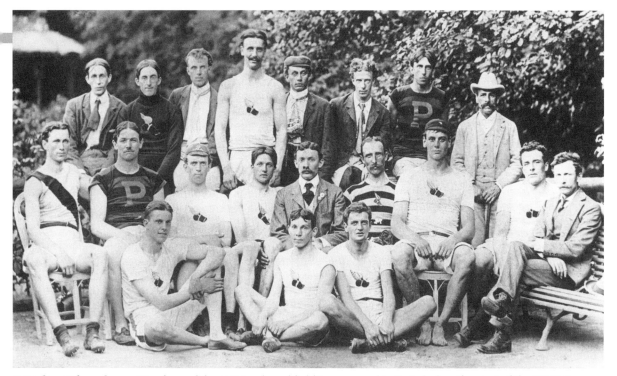

American Olympians *Members of the U.S. track and field team posed in Paris before the start of the 1900 Games.*

domination by American male athletes in the sprint races, winning the 60- and 110-meter races and the 200-meter hurdles. He also won the running long jump.

American A.L. Newton finished the marathon first, but found to his surprise that another runner who had not passed him during the race had already arrived. That racer, Michael Theato, was a Paris native. Theato's knowledge of the city's streets and shortcuts had enabled him to shave off some distance from the 26-mile, 385-yard course. The French judges overlooked his obvious cheating and awarded Theato the gold medal.

One very good thing about de Coubertin's absence was the inclusion of female athletes, whom he had barred from the 1896 competition. The first woman to become an Olympic champion was Great Britain's Charlotte Cooper, who won the tennis singles competition. Women also competed in golf, with American Margaret Abbott winning the nine-hole round with a score of 47.

The competition was also hampered when French organizers scheduled several key finals on a Sunday in July. Many top athletes refused to compete on what they considered to be "the Lord's Day." The French would not move the finals. American Meyer Prinstein ,though Jewish, supported his Christian teammates and refused to compete in the long jump. (He earned a silver medal anyway, thanks to an earlier qualifying jump). Several days later, unofficial competitions were held in events such as the pole vault, where American Daniel Horton's mark would have easily won the official event.

1900

Boxing's First "Match of the Century"

Boxing was a popular spectator sport in the late 1800s and remained so as the new century began. The introduction of standardized rules and the use of padded gloves beginning in the early 1890s had made boxing more of a regular sport than the rough-and-tumble, bare-knuckles brawls featured earlier. Still, boxing in 1900 was a brutal and demanding sport and remained illegal in some parts of the country.

Boxing is divided into weight classes, with fighters of similar weights squaring off against one another. The glamour class is the heavyweights; the actual weight of fighters at this level has changed over the century, but in 1900 it included any boxer of 180 pounds or more.

The heavyweight champion of the era was James J. Jeffries (1875–1953), who won the title in 1899 by knocking out British fighter Robert Fitzsimmons.

In 1900, Jeffries made his third defense of his title against a legendary boxer, "Gentleman" Jim Corbett, who had been the champ from 1892 to 1897. Corbett was a national hero, and many rooted for him in this comeback match against Jeffries, held before 7,000 people on May 11 in New York's Coney Island. The fighters battled through 23 three-minute rounds until Jeffries finally knocked out Corbett. Jeffries remained the heavyweight champion until he retired in 1904.

Over the next few decades, boxing would rise and fall in popularity, often depending on the personalities of its champions, and always fighting against its own brutal nature.

Gibson Girl

By the turn of the century, the idea that women could not take part in athletic competitions was becoming obsolete. Many pockets of resistance remained, not the least of which were other women who felt that such pursuits were "unladylike."

One example from fiction helped spread the idea that femininity could be combined with athleticism. In 1890, illustrator Charles Dana Gibson created the fictional "Gibson Girl." He drew the attractive young woman in a wide variety of sporty settings, including on the golf course (left), on a tennis court, riding horses, and even riding a bicycle. Though several public and private ventures touted the benefits of some sort of exercise for women, seeing the example of this fictitious beauty proved more successful at getting women to give sports a try.

A sports historian in the 1930s wrote, "Gibson did more through his drawings to convince maidens East and West that they wanted to be athletic than any number of health crusades could do."

Vardon Grips America

Golf was beginning to make some inroads into the wider American sports consciousness. But at this point in the century, although more than 1,000 golf courses had been built in the United States, the game still had limited appeal. Golfers needed money to buy gear and to join golf clubs where they could play. Plus, most people did not have the leisure time to get in enough rounds to justify the expense. In addition, the country clubs that grew up around the courses were exclusive outposts of rich society.

In 1900, however, a national tour by Great Britain's Harry Vardon, a famous three-time British Open champion, spurred interest in the game among the general public. The power of the A.G. Spalding Company was behind Vardon's tour. Spalding had been a star baseball player before turning to the sporting goods business, and he was among the first to connect his products with famous athletes such as Vardon. The tour was designed to promote the Vardon Flyer golf ball sold by Spalding. Although Vardon won the 1900 U.S. Open tournament in Chicago in June, the ball was not a big success. Golf, however, enjoyed a little bump in popularity.

The First Davis Cup

Tennis had been played in America for several decades, and British players were still among the world's best, while France had produced several international champions. To spur interest in the game and set up a standard competition among nations, financier Dwight Filley Davis proposed a new annual tournament. Donating the silver trophy, he thus got to name the event the Davis Cup.

The first Davis Cup was played in August in Massachusetts between (all male) teams of American and British players. Davis himself played and won one match, and teammates Malcolm Whitman and Holcombe Ward—both, like Davis, Harvard University men—also won their matches. Weather cancelled the remaining matches, and the U.S. team was declared the winner.

The Davis Cup tournament has been played annually ever since. In 2002, 129 nations competed. The United States has won 32 Davis Cups, the most of any nation. In 1963, the Federation Cup was inaugurated, creating a similar international tournament for female players.

Other Milestones of 1900

✔ Baseball managers Wilbert Robinson and John McGraw, who co-owned a bowling alley in Baltimore, introduced a new sport—duckpins—which uses a smaller ball and pins than is used in bowling. The sport became popular only in a few areas, but remains a local specialty in Baltimore.

✔ The Brooklyn Dodgers won the National League championship in the final year in which the N.L. reigned as the only major league in baseball.

✔ Yale University's perfect 12–0 record earned it the unofficial national college football championship, as selected by the Helms Athletic Foundation.

1901

A New Major League

By the beginning of the 20th century, baseball was far and away the most popular and successful American sport. No other spectator event drew the amount of national and local attention. Thousands of small towns had their own amateur teams, while the 25-year-old National League maintained dominance in the professional ranks . . . until 1901, that is.

Under the leadership of Ban Johnson (1864–1931), the Western League, a "minor" pro league, declared itself a "major" league beginning in 1901, renaming itself the American League. The N.L. had faced off against other rival pro leagues several times in recent decades, including the American Association, which started in 1881 and ended a year later, and the Players' League, formed in 1890 and disbanded in 1892.

Johnson's desire to try again to reach equality with the eight existing N.L. clubs was guided as much by money as anything else. Up until then, N.L. clubs could sign up Western League players without fairly compensating the players' previous teams. Johnson made the battle lines clear by setting up A.L. teams in the same cities as three N.L. teams (Philadelphia, Boston, and Chicago). He and other A.L. team owners (Johnson owned the new Chicago White Stockings) offered some of the N.L. players big contracts to jump to the new league. The first star they corralled was Napoleon Lajoie, a future Hall of Fame second baseman. For a then-enormous salary of $3,500, "Nap" joined the new Philadelphia Athletics and was the first A.L. batting champion at .422.

By the end of the eight-team A.L.'s first season, it had nearly matched the N.L. in attendance. The Pittsburgh Pirates won the N.L. title (the first of three in succession), and the Athletics claimed the first A.L. crown.

Another key development was the creation of the National Association of Professional Baseball Leagues. This group gathered under one flag all the many minor leagues scattered throughout the East, South, and Midwest. The organization set limits on where teams could go for players, awarding each team a certain geographic territory. It also set up the first system for the major league clubs to draft or select players from the minor leagues. The National Association still exists as the governing body of the minor leagues.

McGraw and Tokohoma

Baseball's new American League, like the established National League, did not allow men of color to take part. The ban was not official, but is was real. A few African Americans had played for N.L. clubs in the 1880s, notably catcher Moses Fleetwood Walker, but they were all gone by 1890.

Not all participants in baseball agreed with this racist stance, however. In 1901, New York Giants manager John McGraw, eager for any baseball talent regardless of a player's race, tried to get around the ban. He brought second baseman Charlie Grant, whom he had seen play with a hotel team, to preseason spring training in Arkansas. McGraw called the young hitter Charlie Tokohama, intending to present the African-American Grant as a Native American. N.L. president Charles Comiskey, however, made it clear that the trick would not work, and Grant was not allowed to play.

Women's Hoops Is Born

Unlike most sports, which developed over time, basketball was invented in an afternoon by one man. In 1891, James Naismith (1861–1939), a YMCA teacher in Springfield, Massachusetts, invented the game as a way for his students to stay active indoors in the winter. He wrote up the first 13 rules of the game in December of that year, and they remain remarkably unchanged to this day. Naismith used a soccer ball and a pair of peach baskets as equipment for the first game. (The per-

Baseball Pioneer *This plaque from the Baseball Hall of Fame honors "Ban" Johnson, founder of the American League.*

son who had the bright idea of taking the bottom out of the peach baskets some 15 or so years later remains an unknown hero.)

Through the network of YMCAs and Amateur Athletic Union (AAU) member clubs, basketball spread quickly. By the end of its first decade, basketball was

Other Milestones of 1901

✔ The American League got off to a record-setting start. In one of the first games of the league's history, one team set a record that still stands. On April 25, the Detroit Tigers trailed 13–4 going into the bottom of the ninth inning against the Milwaukee Brewers. Amazingly, they scored 10 runs in the bottom of the ninth to win 14–13. It remains the greatest final-inning comeback in Major League Baseball history.

✔ British America's Cup challenger *Shamrock II*, owned by tea magnate Sir Thomas Lipton, lost to U.S. yacht *Columbia*, continuing a 50-year winning streak by American yachts in the biannual race, held in July.

✔ The University of Michigan finished with an 11–0 record and was named the top college football team in the nation. It was the first time that a Western school won the title over more established Eastern teams.

✔ The American Bowling Congress held its first national tournament in Chicago in September.

Field Hockey Arrives

Another sport that became popular among female athletes made its American debut in 1901. A British teacher named Constance Applebee (1873–1981) was teaching a seminar at Vassar University. There she introduced field hockey, a game already played in many European countries. (Field hockey is played much like ice hockey, except players use curved wooden sticks and a hard rubber ball on a grass field.) Soon other women's colleges invited her to come and teach them the game.

Applebee later established field hockey summer camps and published the first woman's sports magazine (*The Sportswoman*, first issued in 1922). She coached until she was 95 years old.

Major Taylor

Not long after the Civil War, a new sporting craze swept American cities: bicycling. In 1890, advances in making rubber led to air-filled tires, which, along with the development of more durable chains and sprockets, helped create the first "safety bikes." Now much more comfortable (and soon more affordable, thanks to numerous bicycle makers, including a pair of brothers in Ohio who later gained fame in another area of transportation—perhaps you have heard of the Wright Brothers?), bicycles filled city streets.

Naturally, people quickly thought of racing bicycles. In the late 1890s and early 1900s, bike racing was among the most popular spectator sports, with fans filling

played in dozens of colleges, and national championships had been held.

In 1901, Senda Berenson of Smith College recognized the sport as a way for students at her all-female college to get some exercise. Smith defeated Bryn Mawr 4–3 in March in the first women's intercollegiate basketball game.

In those days, the rules of the women's game were quite different. The court was divided into three sections, and players were not allowed to run out of their designated section. This idea was to keep the young women from becoming overexerted, as the tradition of the day dictated.

arenas to watch racers ride at high speeds around high-banked wooden ovals.

In a time when few minorities played important roles in any area of public life, the most famous bicycle racer in America from 1898 to 1904 was an African-American athlete named Marshall W. "Major" Taylor. In 1899, Taylor set numerous world speed records at distances from one-quarter mile to two miles. He did well in an odd type of race held in this era: the six-day indoor bike race.

Taylor not only battled against competitors on the track—literally, sometimes fighting off blows or other physical intimidation—but also against crowds arrayed against him because of his skin color. But over the course of only a few years, he defeated all of these opponents. We can see in Taylor the example of the first black celebrity athlete.

In 1899, Taylor won the world championship in the prestigious one-mile race and later set a world record at that distance. In 1900, he became the overall American sprint champion. Beginning in 1901, he traveled to Europe, Australia, New Zealand, and other countries, meeting and often defeating local champions.

The sad coda to Taylor's story says more about the times than about his skills as a racer. After retiring from racing 1910, failed business ventures cost him his racing winnings and later his marriage. By 1930, he was living in a men's shelter in Chicago and died at age 53 in 1932, virtually unremembered. In recent years, Taylor's story has been revived, with several books about his life being published. Taylor's story was one of both success and sadness.

Speed Racer   *Cyclist Major Taylor excelled at both long and short races, breaking records and winning many world titles.*

1902

First Rose Bowl Game

During the 1901 college football season, the University of Michigan Wolverines outscored their opponents by a stunning total score of 501 to 0. It was the first of four consecutive undefeated seasons for Michigan—the first school not from the East coast of the United States to achieve such gridiron dominance ("gridiron" is a nickname for the football field). Coach Fielding Yost was the driving force behind the Wolverines, while the key player was halfback William Heston, who scored 93 touchdowns in his four seasons at Michigan.

Following the 1901 season, and hoping to expand continued interest in football in the western United States, the organizers of an annual civic celebration in Pasadena, California, made an invitation that would eventually have a huge impact on college football. Up until that time, college teams ended their seasons in late November or early December, with no postseason games. But the Tournament of Roses organizers in Pasadena had the idea to invite mighty Michigan to travel west and play in a special game against a top western team, Stanford University.

The first Rose Bowl game was played on January 1 as part of Pasadena's annual Tournament of Roses, which also included a parade, flower exhibitions, and entertainment. Michigan kept its scoring streak going, wiping out Stanford 49–0. The defeat was so huge that tournament organizers did not have another Rose Bowl game until 1916. However, the idea of a game between champions or rivals from different parts of the country led to

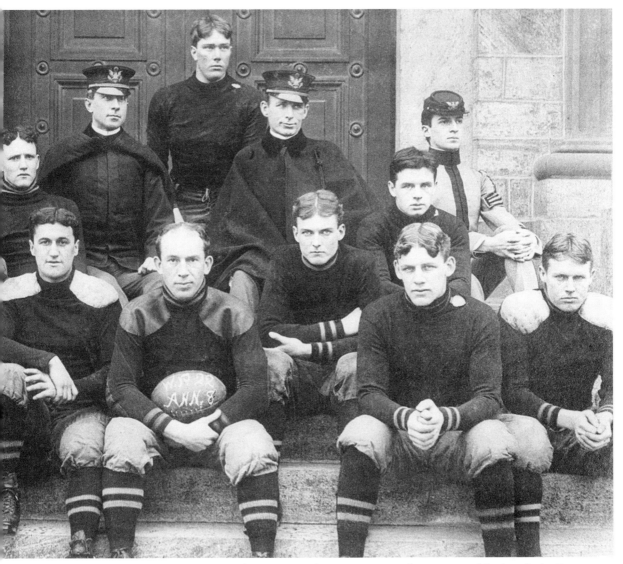

Another Top Team *While Michigan won the West, Army's team at West Point was one of the best in the East.*

the profusion of postseason bowl games that both thrill and bedevil college football today. The now-annual Rose Bowl pits the winner of the Pac Ten Conference on the West Coast against the winner of the Big Ten, made up of Midwestern colleges.

Yost's "point-a-minute" team (so called for its awesome scoring power) continued its streak in the 1902 regular season,

when the Wolverines outscored their opponents 644-12 while winning 11 straight games and the national championship.

Ping-Pong Goes National!

The combination of a new type of sports equipment and a book turned a rarely played English indoor game into

1902

a national craze in 1902. Table tennis, or ping-pong, as it came to be known in the United States thanks to a toy manufacturers' product, began in England in the 1880s using a rubber ball and small paddles on a tabletop. In 1900, the invention of a lightweight, plant-based fiber product called celluloid radically changed the new game. Using small, light balls made of sturdy yet inexpensive celluloid, table tennis began to spread rapidly. It was greatly encouraged with the publication of a book by a British player named Arnold "Ping-Pong" Parker—*Ping-Pong: The Game and How to Play It.*

After capturing the public's fancy for a year or two, ping-pong faded a bit, but it remains a popular pastime in game rooms and basements across America. In some countries, such as China, Taiwan, and other Asian nations, table tennis is played by many millions and with great success in international competition. In 1971, President Richard Nixon used a tour by American ping-pong players to China to reopen diplomatic relations severed decades earlier.

Top Tennis Ace

The first national championship of men's tennis in the United States was held in 1881 (the first women's championship was held six years later). Dick Sears won the first seven championships, a total matched by only two men since: fellow International Tennis Hall of Fame members William Larned and Bill Tilden. Larned (1872–1926) was a tall, righthanded man from New Jersey who was America's top tennis star of the early 1900s. He began his successful career on the court by winning the 1892 college national championship while at Cornell University.

Larned was 28 when he won the first of his U.S. championships in 1901; he repeated in 1902. In 1907, he won again, beginning a string of five straight national titles. Larned also was part of six Davis Cup teams, helping the United States win in 1902. Except for a stint in the Army during the Spanish-American War in 1898, Larned was ranked in the top 10 nationally—including number one eight times—for 20 years.

The top female champion of this era was Elisabeth Moore, who made the finals of the championship every year from 1901 through 1905, winning three times.

Other Milestones of 1902

✔ A quartet of Harvard runners set a new world record in the mile relay race, finishing in three minutes, 21.2 seconds.

✔ The U.S. team won the second Davis Cup tennis competition over the British team; the event was not held in 1902.

✔ The debate over amateur versus pro athletes continued in the sport of track. In April, Arthur Duffey ran a 100-yard dash in 9.6 seconds, a new record. However, in 1905, his record was taken away on the grounds that he had earlier become a "professional."

✔ Ralph "Socks" Seybold of baseball's Philadelphia Athletics slugged 16 home runs to lead the American League, a record that stood until 1919, when Babe Ruth hit 29.

Early Pro Football

The birth of what would become today's National Football League would not come for another 18 years, but the popularity of college football led some to give pro football a try. In 1902, along with other athletic clubs, a pair of Major League Baseball organizations formed pro football teams. The Philadelphia Athletics and Philadelphia Phillies both put together squads of former collegians and paid them a small salary to be part of what they called the National Football League (the current NFL does not recognize this group as its ancestor). On November 21, the Athletics won the first night football game ever played, defeating an amateur team from Elmira, New York, 39–0. Some of the well-known baseball players who tried their hand at this sport included future Hall of Fame pitchers Christy Mathewson of the Giants and Rube Waddell of the Athletics.

In December, a five-team series of games was held at New York's Madison Square Garden, making them the first indoor football games. A team from Syracuse, New York, led by future coaching legend Glenn "Pop" Warner, won the event. The World Series, as it was known, was only held one more time, in 1903, and the pro league disbanded shortly after.

1903

Harvard Stadium Opens

The growing popularity of college football led in this decade to the creation of several enormous stadiums designed to hold the growing crowds. As was also the case with baseball stadiums (see page 54), new engineering techniques using concrete and steel greatly influenced the size and style of these new sporting venues.

In 1903, Harvard Stadium opened in Cambridge, Massachusetts, as the first all-concrete stadium in the country. Harvard was a perennial powerhouse in college football, finishing undefeated in 1901, and it drew large and enthusiastic crowds. On November 14, however, the fans at the brand-new stadium went home disappointed as Dartmouth College spoiled the opening of the stadium by knocking off the home team 11–0.

African Americans in Baseball

As mentioned earlier, baseball's major leagues barred African-American players from playing on their teams. But this did not mean that black athletes were unable to play the game. Many semi-pro and amateur teams were integrated. And some top black teams played exhibition games against teams made up of white major league players.

Beginning in the late 1800s, several all-black professional teams were formed; in 1887 the League of Colored Professional Base Ball Clubs was established with teams in nine cities. It lasted only a year.

As the 1900s began, several African-American teams played baseball as well as any all-white major league team, according to many observers. These black teams played against one another in loosely organized leagues and held an annual championship. In 1903, the winners were the Cuban X-Giants, who defeated the Philadelphia Giants four games to one. In that series, Philadelphia's Dan McClelland pitched a perfect game, the first by a black pitcher. (A perfect game is one in which the pitcher works all nine innings and does not allow a single opponent to reach base by any means.)

Dozens of all-black teams continued to play against one another in ballparks large and small for the next two decades, but their organization was somewhat

Clear the Field! *Fans crowded the diamond before the first game of the 1903 World Series (page 25).*

haphazard. By 1920, however, led by men such as Rube Foster (see below), Negro League baseball, as these teams came to be collectively known , had become successful, organized enterprises. The Negro Leagues were especially popular with African-American fans, who filled some ballparks into which they were not allowed to enter to watch white teams.

Rube Foster

In 1971, the National Baseball Hall of Fame in Cooperstown, New York, created a special committee to look into the history of the Negro Leagues and de-termine which of its many talented players should be elected as full members of the Hall. In 1981, this commission chose Andrew "Rube" Foster (1878–1930) to join the ranks of the greatest baseball players of all time.

Foster, a native of Texas, was one of the most dominant players and personalities in the history of African-American organized baseball. Some historians say his impact was so great that he should be called "the father of the Negro Leagues." He was an outstanding pitcher and joined a pro team in Waco, Texas, in 1896 after finishing the eighth grade. In 1902, after moving to the more competitive

1903

Cuban X-Giants, he won an exhibition game pitching against famed Philadelphia Athletics pitcher Rube Waddell, thus earning his lifelong nickname.

In 1903, Foster joined the Philadelphia-based X-Giants and won an astounding 54 games while losing only one. His pitching was key to the team's national championship that year. After playing for several other teams in the coming years, Foster became a manager and later an owner of several clubs, including the 1907 Leland Giants, which finished 110–10 that season, and the 1914 and 1917 champion Chicago American Giants.

In 1919, Foster was one of several team owners who helped form the Negro National League; he was elected the league's first president. Baseball historians credit the formation of the league with saving and giving credibility to what had been a disorganized assortment of black teams.

Foster's skills on and off the diamond surely earned him a much-deserved place among the legends of the sport.

Here Comes the Commission

The uneasy coexistence of the American and National Leagues in baseball (see page 14) became more formal before the 1903 season with the creation of the National Commission. Rather than having two separate leagues with different rules and different ways of doing business, the team owners saw the

Baseball Season

Harold Seymour published a trilogy of books, beginning in 1967, that carefully traced the early years of baseball. From his second volume, *The Golden Years* (published in 1971), this passage helps modern readers understand the importance of baseball in America in the early 1900s.

Thus baseball was more than a game for boys in America. It was part of adult society, too. Its terminology infiltrated the language . . . and songs were written about it. Newspapers, sporting-goods stores, railroads, hotels, and other businesses found they had a stake in its success. It was equated with Americanism, democracy, and the health and well-being of the young and old. Morgan Bulkeley [a president of the National League] wrote, "There is nothing which will help quicker and better to amalgamate the foreign born and those born of foreign parents in this country, than to give them the good old-fashioned game of Base Ball." . . . In short, baseball was ingrained in the American psyche. Its importance in the first decades of the twentieth century was astonishing. "We have five seasons," remarked an observer. "Spring, summer, autumn, winter, and the baseball season."

The Heads of Baseball *These members of the "Commission," made up of (left to right) Harry Pulliam, August Herrmann, Ban Johnson, and J.E. Bruce (the group's secretary) ran Major League Baseball.*

wisdom of joining together under one banner. The A.L. had proven by this time to be a success and worthy of matching up with the established N.L.

Under the National Agreement signed by members of both leagues, a three-man National Commission would run what would be called Organized Baseball. Though the A.L. and N.L. continued to play only teams within their own leagues during the season (see "The First World Series," following), the new agreement kept the clubs from raiding one another for talent and from moving into one another's territory.

This joint supervision of the two major leagues remained in force for the next century, with several notable modifications along the way. The most important was the switch from a three-man commission to a single all-powerful commissioner in 1920.

The First World Series

Following the 1903 baseball season, the champions of the American and National leagues faced off in a postseason championship for the first time. A late-September agreement between Harry Killelea, owner of the A.L.'s Boston Pilgrims (later the Red Sox) and Barney Dreyfuss, owner of the N.L.'s Pittsburg (it was spelled without the final "h" in those days) Pirates led to the first World Series.

Now a century old, the World Series was a hit from the beginning. More than 10,000 people surrounded Boston's Huntington Avenue Grounds for the first game, played on October 1. So many fans spilled onto the grounds that ropes were used to hold them back in the outfield, necessitating special ground rules for balls hit into the crowds on the edges of the field.

1903

The locals expected their team, led by pitchers Cy Young and Bill Dineen, to win easily, while the more-established Pirates had the honor of the N.L. to uphold and faced tremendous pressure from other N.L. teams to win.

The first game of the best-of-nine series went to Pittsburg, with outfielder Jimmy Sebring hitting the first home run in World Series history to back the pitch-ing of Deacon Phillippe. Boston won the second game, but the Pirates won two more, with Phillippe getting both victories. However, Young and Dineen both pitched a pair of complete-game victories in the next four games, and Boston won the Series five games to three.

The Boston victory had great reso-nance in the baseball community. Much to the surprise of N.L. supporters, the "new"

Cy Young

Pitching for Boston in that first World Series was one of the greatest baseball players of all time. Denton True "Cy" Young remains the sport's all-time leader with 511 wins. No other pitcher is within 100 wins of that total. In a 19-year career with three teams, Young set a remarkable standard for future pitchers.

Young earned his famous nickname in one of two ways (experts disagree). The first is based on his rural upbringing in Ohio; "Cyrus" or "Cy" was a slightly derogatory nickname for a country boy among baseball's big-city ballplayers. The second leg-end is that his fastball was so devastating that he broke boards in fences, much as a cyclone might have done. In any case, his outstanding pitching achievements—which included the century's first major-league perfect game in 1904 (see page 28)—made him one of the first players inducted into the Hall of Fame when it opened in 1936. In addi-tion, when baseball instituted an annual award for the top pitcher in each league, it named the award for him. To be a Cy Young Award winner is to be named a pitcher who approaches, but probably can never top, Cy Young himself.

Other Milestones of 1903

✔ The International Hockey League was formed in Michigan. It was the first pro ice hockey league in the United States. The Portage Lakers won the first title in March.

✔ *Shamrock III* lost to U.S. yacht *Reliance* in the America's Cup competition in September. It was Sir Thomas Lipton's third of five unsuccessful attempts to win the Cup. In fact, the America's Cup remained in American hands until Australia won in 1983.

✔ On June 15, Barney Oldfield became the first man to drive a racecar faster than a mile a minute (60 mph).

✔ In the space of a week in August, "Iron" Joe McGinnity, a pitcher for baseball's New York Giants, twice pitched in and won both games of a doubleheader.

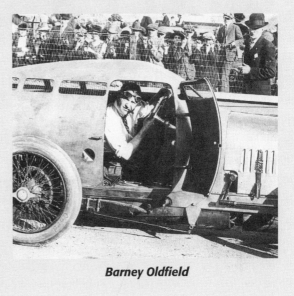

Barney Oldfield

A.L. had proven more than the equal of the older N.L. champion. The legitimacy of the World Series (sometimes called the World's Series in those early days) was \unquestioned (by most, at least; see page 32). Boston's championship also helped solidify the "Fall Classic" in the American consciousness. Over the next century, the event became the site of numerous historic events, the linchpin of an annual love affair with a sport, and a continuing American tradition that has held sway far beyond the confines of the sports pages.

1904

Cy Young's Perfect Game

Already a World Series champion, Cy Young added another achievement to his career on May 5 by pitching the first perfect game of the century in the major leagues. The first two perfect games were pitched, remarkably, five days apart in 1880 by John Lee Richmond and John M. Ward, but no one did it again for 25 years . . . until Young. In the 120-plus years of professional baseball, only 17 such games have been pitched. Young's was the first under the modern rules of baseball.

Facing the Philadelphia Athletics, Young was masterful that day. Pitching at home before the Boston Pilgrims' largest crowd of the season, Young mowed down opposing batters like he was chopping wood back home in Pennsylvania.

Young got some defensive help when right fielder Buck Freeman made a nice running catch and catcher Lou Criger went to the edge of the field to catch a foul pop-up. In the world of baseball in those days, a perfect day by the defense was nearly as rare as a perfect day by the pitcher.

Young's teammates also helped him by scoring three runs. Young himself contributed to the third run, which scored when the Athletics made an error fielding his ground ball in the seventh inning. As the ninth inning began, the crowd, according to contemporary accounts, was extremely excited. They knew they were watching a no-hitter, but few probably realized the significance of the game. It had been a quarter-century since something like this had happened; in fact, it would not be until 1922 that such a feat was called a perfect game.

Young retired the side for the ninth time, and the game was over. The crowd of more than 10,000 spilled onto the field, trying to carry their hero off on their shoulders. The *Boston Post* called it "the most wonderful game of ball in the annals of American sport." The nine innings of perfection were also part of a 45-inning streak in which Young did not allow a run, a record that stood for two decades until it was broken in 1924 by Walter Johnson. (The current mark is 59 innings, set in 1988 by Orel Hershiser.)

An American Olympics

In 1904, the Olympic Games were held for the first time in the United States. Unfortunately, Olympic historians

A Mighty Champ *Irish-American strong man Martin Sheridan won the discus throw at the 1900 and 1904 Olympics, though in 1904, he had little international competition.*

are nearly unanimous in calling these Games the worst of the modern era.

Four years earlier, Pierre de Coubertin of the IOC (see page 10) decided the 1904 Games should be held in the United States. Several cities, including Chicago, St. Louis, and Buffalo, New York, vied for the honor. In 1901, the Chicago organizers got the news that they had won the right to host the Games.

1904

Then the trouble started. A massive exposition was being planned for that summer in St. Louis to honor the 100th anniversary of the Louisiana Purchase. The St. Louis organizers objected to Chicago having a large international event during the same time as their own, and they began to lobby hard to have the Olympics take place under the auspices of the Louisiana Purchase Exposition. Not only that, but the IOC worried that their still-new Olympic Games might be lost amid the busy summer events in the Midwest. As a result, in 1903 they changed their minds and gave the Games to St. Louis. It was a decision they would come to regret.

The Exposition organizers hired famed sportsman James Sullivan (1860–1914), president of the Amateur Athletic Union, to come to St. Louis and take charge of the Olympics, which, as expected, were now to be held within the larger Exposition. Sullivan took his duties a bit too literally and staged more than 40 athletic events of all types throughout the summer, calling all of them "Olympic" and creating confusion that still trickles down through the Olympic record book. He began the Games with a high school football tournament and included such oddities as roque, a form of croquet; Irish games such as hurling; a game between two Native American schools in football; and track meets for local youngsters.

The more traditional Olympic sports were also contested, including swimming, track and field, fencing, and gymnastics. However, very few foreign teams chose to take part, thus turning the 1904 Games into little more than an American sports festival. The track and field competition had so few international athletes that several U.S. cities and athletic clubs sent "teams" to compete. The shotput was won by John Flanagan, representing not America, but the Greater New York Irish American Athletic Club. Swimming had only four nations competing, while in gym-

A Savage Display

And event that ran concurrent with the 1904 Olympics highlighted how many people in America and Europe looked upon the native peoples of the world as second-class citizens, both culturally and physically. To add to the "exposition" nature of the Louisiana Purchase Exposition, the organizers created an affair that today would be met with horror. "Anthropological Days" was a gathering of live native people from many lands who were literally put on display for fair-goers to look at. Pygmies from Africa, Native Americans from Canada and Mexico, tribal people from the Philippines, and many others (including the Apache chief Geronimo), were brought to the United States for the event.

To make the event more bizarre, on August 12 and 13 AAU president James Sullivan brought out the various native people and asked them to take part in random athletic events. Not surprisingly, they did not perform very well in contests that were wholly unfamiliar to them. Said Sullivan afterward, the events "were only successful in that they were destructive of the common belief that the greatest natural athletes were to be found among the uncivilized tribes of the world."

To his credit, Pierre de Coubertin (who did not attend any part of the St. Louis Games), lambasted the exhibition. "In no place but America would one have dared to place such events on a program, but to Americans anything is permissible." He called Anthropology Days an "outrageous charade."

nastics, Austria and Switzerland each sent one athlete to join those from America and Great Britain as the only competitors. Most nations objected to the cost of sending teams to the United States, but the patriotic aspects of Sullivan's promotion of the Games also put off some teams. In the end, U.S. athletes won 75 gold medals. Coming in second was Cuba, with five.

Another unique aspect of the 1904 Game was Sullivan's ongoing "salesmanship" of the sporting lifestyle that his AAU preached. "The sound body is the safest guardian of morality and of civilization," he wrote in 1904. "So agree teachers and philosophers as well as physicians. The first decade of the new century finds the world ready to actively support the movement toward intelligent physical training, the principal avenue to which is sane competitive athletics." Sullivan paired the American ideal of participation and physical activity with the idea of moral strength, a not-unusual sentiment for the age and one of the principles behind de Coubertin's Olympic movement.

The Olympic Games themselves, such as they were, did generate some athletic highlights, such as the continued jumping success of Ray Ewry, who won three more gold medals to add to the ones he got in 1900, and the swimming prowess of Charles Daniels (see page 40), who won the 200- and 400-meter freestyle swimming races. Another positive note was the presence of several African-American athletes, including George Poage, whose bronze medals in the hurdles were the first ever won by a black athlete. Joseph Stadler, also African American, won medals in jumping competitions.

Some Advice for Active Women

The continuing availability of leisure time to a growing crop of middle-class Americans led to articles and books extolling the virtues of exercise, especially for women. Here is one example from the July 10, 1904, edition of the *Los Angeles Times*, which also suggested women walk up hills, go fishing, and ride horses:

> Let milady take a row over the placid stream in a boat, remaining out some hours, and she will discover on her return to shore that the bracing air and exercise undergone, will make a "new woman" of her, her health being restored.

Along with the public relations disaster of the accompanying "Anthropological Days" (see the box opposite), the thoroughly un-Olympic nature of the St. Louis event gave the IOC all the power it needed to make sure that it maintained control of future Olympic Games. So while St. Louis can be seen as a sporting low for the Olympic movement, it also helped to create the international success story that continues today.

First Gold Cup Race

Americans, it was quickly becoming clear, would race anything. Horses, of course, were on the track from the earliest days of the republic. When bicycles were invented, racing them became a sport very quickly.

Meanwhile, the first the first major powerboat race, the Gold Cup held by the American Powerboat Association, was held in June on New York's Hudson River.

1904

A 59-foot boat named *Standard* roared home a winner at the then-fast speed of more than 23 miles per hour. C.C. Ricotte was the first winning pilot. The Gold Cup is still contested today by boats in a wide variety of size, weight, and engine capacity categories.

No World Series!

Although the 1903 World Series had been a giant success, the New York Giants put a temporary hold on the event in 1904. Following their N.L. championship, the team, led by president John T. Brush and manager John McGraw (see box below), refused to play against the A.L. champion Boston Pilgrims.

The temperamental McGraw took the stage at a celebration of the team's pennant and announced the decision, castigating the Boston team as playing in a "minor league." The real reason for the Giants' refusal stemmed from McGraw's

John McGraw

As both a player and a manager, John McGraw (1873–1934) was among the most controversial and influential figures in early pro baseball. He began his career in 1891 as a player with the Baltimore Orioles, then of the minor league American Association. Though small at 5 feet, 7 inches, McGraw was one of the toughest players of the day and one not averse to bending the rules to get ahead. He helped the Orioles win three league titles and then became the team's manager, while also playing third base.

When Ban Johnson started the American League in 1901, he called on McGraw to lead the new Baltimore A.L. team, also called the Orioles. However, after McGraw got into one too many arguments with umpires, Johnson suspended him. McGraw moved on in 1902 to become manager of the New York Giants, with whom he had his greatest success. His 1905 Giants won the World Series, and New York won National League pennants four other times through 1917. The Giants began another great run in 1921 with the first of two straight World Series titles and four straight N.L. championships.

The man sometimes called "Little Napoleon" for his belligerent, dictatorial style was as well known for his constant arguments with umpires as for his managerial leadership. He was inducted into the Baseball Hall of Fame in 1936.

John McGraw

Other Milestones of 1904

✔ Charles Follis became the first African-American professional football player when he joined the American Professional Football Association's Shelby (Ohio) Blues.

✔ The National Ski Association was formed in Michigan on February 21.

✔ The National League's Brooklyn Superbas played host to the Boston Beaneaters on Sunday, April 17. It was the first Sunday baseball game played in New York, which, like other cities, had various regulations (known as "blue laws") banning play on Sundays. The teams got around the ban by not charging spectators admission; however, fans had to buy scorecards to get into the ballpark.

✔ The New York Highlanders' Jack Chesbro completed his first 30 starts en route to pitching 48 complete games. Modern baseball pitchers might pitch only two or three such games in a season. Chesbro's record is one that will almost certainly never be broken.

---

and Brush's hatred of A.L. president and founder Ban Johnson, who had been McGraw's boss when McGraw was the manager of the Baltimore Orioles.

Boston fans were outraged, of course, and claimed that McGraw and his team were afraid to face them. McGraw, in his legendary haughtiness, ignored the pleas and printed up "World's Champion" jerseys that his team wore while taking the field for the 1905 season.

Cooler heads prevailed, however, and the National Commission put in place what would eventually be called the Brush Rules—named after the Giants' reluctant owner—to avoid such a situation in the future. The new rules stated that the two league champions had to meet in a post-season series to determine an overall champion.

The World Series was not cancelled again until 1994, because of a labor dispute between players and owners.

Barney's Dragon

As motor vehicles of all sorts began to be built, people raced them. The old saying in racing is that the first automobile race began on the day the second car was built. This was despite the fact that very few people owned cars or, in some places, had even seen one.

Traveling troops of racers took their cars to fairgrounds and races around the East. On October 8, George Heath won the first Vanderbilt Cup race, averaging 52 miles per hour. On October 29, Barney Oldfield, driving his Green Dragon car, defeated several European challengers to win the Empire City race in Yonkers, New York. Oldfield was the most famous of the new breed of auto racers, challenging speed and daring death in what were then "newfangled" machines. The popularity of auto racing continued to grow dramatically through the coming decades.

1905

Soccer Kicks Off

🏆 Soccer grew out of various ball-kicking games developed in Britain in the mid-1800s. The rules were first codified in 1863. European immigrants brought the game to America, where the more-familiar American form of football (as soccer is called everywhere but the United States) was played. (Trivia fans will enjoy knowing how soccer got its name. The original name was "association football." Association is abbreviated "assoc." From that came the nickname soccer.)

Soccer in America was a minor sport, played by immigrant communities and few Americans. The German community in St. Louis, for instance, sponsored dozens of teams and produced some of the first great American players. However, as American football continued to face serious challenges relating to its violence and danger (see page 41 for more on changes afoot in college football), the relatively safer sport of soccer began to look more appealing.

In 1905, the Intercollegiate Soccer Association was founded by five East Coast schools. Haverford (Pennsylvania) College defeated Harvard 1–0 in April 1905 in the first ISA game. Haverford was the first college to form a soccer team, followed by the Crimson of Harvard. Columbia University students formed a team amid opposition that it would take attention away from the more popular American football. At Cornell University, the game was spread by foreign students, including a Dutch player who was the school's first team captain.

In 1907, reflecting on the state of the game following the first two years of ISA play, the Spalding Athletic Guide wrote, "Association football has made more rapid strides the last three years in our American colleges than any other sport. . . . 'Soccer' will make steady progress and become more and more a factor in college sport. The game is fast and clean, and it offers a chance for light, clever, sturdy young men or for the average college man." The guide went on to say that "there are not wanting many indications that it will soon become a popular scholastic sport."

Events in the coming years, however, notably the reorganization and rapid rise of American college football and a backlash against games perceived as "immigrant" or "foreign," soon relegated soccer to the low levels of popularity it suffered

Tiger Cub *Ty Cobb is a young man in this 1905 photo, as he began one of baseball's greatest playing careers.*

in the United States until near the end of the 20th century.

Ty Cobb's Auspicious Start

On August 30, a young man from Georgia smacked a double in his first major league at-bat for the Detroit Tigers. Over the next 23 years, Ty Cobb fashioned one of baseball's most successful careers and become one of its all-time greatest players. He finished his career with 4,191 hits, the most ever at the time and a mark not topped until Pete Rose got his 4,192nd hit in 1985. Cobb's career batting average of .366 remains the

1905

highest, as are his 12 American League batting titles. He was also the all-time leader in stolen bases (until 1982) and in runs (until 2002). His single-season record of 96 stolen bases was the standard until 1962. Cobb combined batting skill and baserunning expertise more than any other player before or since, a style that was perfect for the game at the time. Most teams relied on speed, "small baseball" (lots of little hits rather than big home runs, which were rare), and great pitching.

Unfortunately, Cobb was also equally well known for his terrible temper and fearsome competitiveness. He was famous for sharpening his spikes, the better to try to inflict wounds on fielders guarding the bases he was stealing. He regularly got into arguments with umpires and opposing players. He once fought an umpire on the field after a game and nearly traded punches with the great Babe Ruth. "When I began playing the game," Cobb wrote, "baseball was about as gentlemanly as a kick in the [groin]. I was like a steel spring with a growing and dangerous flaw in it. If it is wound too tight or has the slightest weak point, it will fly apart, then it is done for."

In his most famous display of temper, which led to one of baseball's oddest games, Cobb vaulted into the stands during a 1912 game to battle a fan who was berating him. After Cobb was suspended by the league for his actions, his teammates refused to play without him. They did not show up for the next game, and the Tigers called on a team of amateurs and collegians, losing 24–2. Only when threatened with lifetime expulsion did the Tigers return to the field.

Cobb led Detroit to only one A.L. title, in 1909 (see page 57), but the Tigers lost in the World Series. He became the team's player-manager in 1921, but his fierce style did not work well.

Cobb retired in 1928 and was one of the first players chosen to be in the new Baseball Hall of Fame in 1936. Cobb's legacy of skill on the diamond was clouded by his less-than-savory personality, but his place among baseball's greatest is well deserved.

Masterful Mathewson

Another all-time baseball superstar put on a performance at the 1905 World Series that still ranks among the greatest feats in baseball history. Christy Mathewson, ace pitcher of the New York Giants, was in the early years of what would also be a Hall of Fame career. But while Cobb was all spit, nails, and anger, Mathewson was calm, reserve, and prudence. A rarity in baseball, Mathewson had attended college, studying and playing for Cornell University. He was a great all-around athlete as well as what was then considered a gentleman. A devout Baptist, he refused to pitch on Sundays, and he rarely took part in the many legendary postgame parties preferred by many pro players of the day.

Mathewson represented for many fans the exemplar of the athlete. Tall, strong, attractive, well-educated, and supremely talented, he mixed as well with his rougher teammates as he did in "polite society." In a time in which some hotels would not let baseball players stay for fear of their uncouth behavior, Mathewson was a shining light of good manners. He also wrote well enough to work as a sportswriter covering some World Series games, and he published a series of novels for young readers based on the exploits of a fictional high school baseball player.

But back to the World Series. The Giants faced the Boston Pilgrims, champions of the American League, in October. With the Brush Rules in place (see page 33), New York, which had shunned the A.L. champions in 1904, had no choice but to take on the Pilgrims. It was perhaps the best-pitched World Series ever. In the space of six days, Mathewson threw three shutouts while allowing only 14 hits and one walk in 27 innings. He struck out 18 batters. The Giants' Joe McGinnity pitched a shutout for the team's fourth win, and the Giants lost their only game by a shutout, thus creating a unique record of a Series in which every game ended in a shutout for one team or another.

Mathewson was simply remarkable in this World Series. Other pitchers after him went on to win three games in a single Series, but none would match his record of shutout innings, and none would complete their feats in less than a week. Armed with a powerful fastball, a devastating screwball, and the poise and will of a true champion, Mathewson set a new standard for pitchers.

Mathewson's remarkable baseball career continued until 1917, when a call to serve his country in World War I cost him his health and led to his early death (see page 96). His skills and his impact on the game, however, will long be remembered by fans.

A Giant Arm *New York Giants pitcher Christy Mathewson was one of the stellar athletes of the early century, attracting attention as much for his character off the field as for his play on it.*

Michigan's Streak Ends

From 1901 to 1904, the University of Michigan Wolverines football team was nearly unstoppable. They won 43 games, lost none, and tied once. They allowed their opponents in those four seasons a grand total of 40 points, while

An All-Around Sports Success

Few sportsmen had such a large impact on two major sports as Amos Alonzo Stagg (1862–1965) had on both football and basketball. He was present at the creation of the sport of basketball and helped refine and spread the game. As a football coach, he was an innovator whose effects are still felt in today's game.

Stagg started out to be a minister, studying at the Yale Divinity School until his poor sermonizing abilities turned him to other pursuits. Athletics had always been his strong suit, and he found work at the YMCA in Springfield, Massachusetts. In 1891, fellow teacher James Naismith invented basketball, and in early 1892, Stagg took part in the first public exhibition of the game. In fact, Stagg scored the only basket for his team in its 5–1 loss. Moving to the University of Chicago that fall, Stagg became the school's first football coach and head of its new Physical Culture Department.

During his 41 years at Chicago, Stagg instituted a truly remarkable number of football innovations, including the huddle between plays, the center snap, the onside kick, the placekick, and putting men in motion before a play. He invented the tackling dummy, was the first coach to come up with numbered and named plays, and created the idea of awarding college athletes "letters" for

Amos Alonzo Stagg

their achievements. Today, the American Football Coaches Association names its highest annual award for Stagg.

That would be enough for most people, but his contributions to basketball are nearly as numerous. Stagg brought the sport to Chicago with him when he come to work for the school, and he formed the first intercollegiate basketball tournament. He created the now-standard arrangement of five players on a team and led his Chicago Maroons to seven Big Ten basketball titles. His achievements earned him election to the Naismith Memorial Basketball Hall of Fame in 1959.

But wait, as they say in TV commercials, there is more: Stagg also coached the Chicago baseball team to six league championships. He led the track team that competed in the 1900 Olympics in Paris. He coached several track athletes at the 1924 Olympics. And he was on the U.S. Olympic Committee for nearly 30 years.

After moving to the University of the Pacific in 1946 and then "retiring," Stagg coached with his son at Pennsylvania's Susquehenna University for another dozen years, followed by a coaching stint at a junior college in California. He coached until he was 98 years old, racking up a then-record total of 314 victories in football.

scoring more than 2,000 points them-selves. Entering the 1905 season, there was no reason to think things would be different. And until November 24, they were not. Michigan steamrolled through the season, outscoring its opponents 495 to 0 and winning 11 straight games. Then came Thanksgiving.

The University of Chicago team had matched Michigan victory for victory in 1905. Led by famed coach Amos Alonzo Stagg (see the box opposite) and out-standing kicker Walter Eckersall, Chicago came into the Thanksgiving showdown also undefeated. The winner of the game would probably be named the national champion. The last time Michigan had lost, in fact, had been to Chicago, way back in 1900.

Unlike most of the two teams' other games, this contest was a defensive strug-gle. Neither team could mount much of an attack, and field position became the key to the game. No one scored until the fourth quarter, when Eckersall sailed a punt into Michigan's end zone. Michigan's Dan Clark fielded the punt and tried to run it out of the end zone, but he was tackled there. The result was a safety, worth two points to Chicago. That was all the scoring Michigan would allow that day (in fact, all season), but it was enough to hand the

Wolverines their first loss in five sea-sons—Chicago held Michigan scoreless. Stagg's Maroons had defeated the "point-a-minute" Wolverines and earned the school's first national college football championship.

Other Milestones of 1905

✔ The love-hate battle in college sports continued when Columbia University banned all intercollegiate sports except row-ing. As more and more students wanted to take part in athlet-ics of various kinds, sometimes to the detriment of their studies, some college administrators debated the role of sports in col-lege life.

✔ In ice hockey, the red line was first used at the center of the rink this season. This line runs across the center of the rink, widthwise, and at the time it divided it into offensive and de-fensive halves. Players were not allowed to precede the puck into their offensive half; if they did, they would be called for being offside.

✔ In golf, Willie Anderson won his third consecutive U.S. Open in June.

✔ After heavyweight boxing champion James Jeffries retired, top contenders Marvin Hart and Jack Root met on July 3 to claim the vacant title. Hart won in 12 rounds and became the new heavyweight champ.

1906

Pool Shark

🏆 On January 15, Willie Hoppe (1887–1959) took the first dramatic step in a sporting career that was one of the most dominant of the century. Hoppe's sport was billiards, and in Paris that day he won the first world championship of his career at the age of just 18. Hoppe had been playing billiards since he was five years old, and was a pro by the time he was 14. His victory in 1906 began a remarkable run of world championships. Except for 1907, 1912, and 1913, he reigned as the world champion until 1925! In 1927, the world tournament changed its format, from a type of billiards called balkline to one known as three-cushion. Changing gears swiftly, Hoppe was the world champ again in 1936, the first of 12 world three-cushion titles (including six in a row from 1947 to 1952) he won before retiring after 1952.

America's Swimming Star

🏆 A loss helped turn Charles Daniels (1885–1973) into the greatest swimming success story of the first decade of the 20th century. His success helped propel the United States into a century of dominance at the highest levels of international swimming competitions.

By the time of a loss in 1905 to Scott Leary, Daniels was already a champion, having won gold medals in the 200- and 400-meter freestyle swims at the 1904 Olympics in St. Louis. But after watching Leary finish ahead of him with a type of swimming stroke called the Australian crawl, Daniels adopted the style and improved it. His new "American crawl" found the swimmer kicking six times for every head turn to breathe, and he used it to great effect. Daniels won the 1906 and 1908 Olympic 100-meter championships. In all his Olympic competition, Daniels won four gold medals, a mark that stood until Don Schollander topped it in 1968.

In 1906, Daniels had one of his greatest years. Along with his Olympic triumph, he became, on February 26, the first American to swim 100 meters in less than a minute. In March, he set a world record of 57.6 seconds at the distance and lowered it twice more in the coming years. From 1904 to 1911, Daniels won an astounding 33 individual swimming championships in a wide variety of distances, from sprints to as much as a mile.

Dangerous Formation *This "flying wedge" formation was one of the reasons for the reform of college football.*

Teddy Rides Rough on Football

In late 1905, the President of the United States stepped into a national sporting controversy for the first time when Theodore Roosevelt called for a ban on college football. Roosevelt was not alone in his worries about a game that was becoming increasingly violent and deadly.

In the 1905 season alone, 18 players died as a result of injuries on the field. Players wore little or no padding, and helmets (which many players did not wear) were little more than thin leather coverings. Plays such as the flying wedge, in which a ballcarrier was almost carried down the field by a tightly packed group of teammates, helped cause many of the injuries. In addition, the higher and higher salaries offered to top coaches were offending many in the academic establishment, while players were being openly recruited and essentially bribed to go to certain schools. Other players were playing after their legal years of playing time had been used up.

Roosevelt gathered leaders from top Eastern colleges and demanded that they fix the game or stop it entirely. He was certainly in favor of athletics in general, and his influence on the physical, active culture of the day was large. But, as James Day, the chancellor of Syracuse University said, "One human life is too big a price to pay for all the games of the season."

1906

What was needed, said reformers, was a national organizing group to control how college football was played and governed. Several meetings were held in late 1905. By March of 1906, it was official: the Intercollegiate Athletic Association of the United States (IAAUS) was born, with more than 60 members. By 1910, it had grown to include more than 100 schools and had gained the name by which it is known today: the National Collegiate Athletic Association (NCAA).

The initial challenge, however, remained: Fix college football. Among the first items the group agreed to was the introduction of the forward pass. Previous-ly, players could only pass the ball backward (called a lateral). By allowing players to throw the ball downfield, the game was instantly made more open and free-flowing. In addition, the distance for a first down went from five yards to 10, making dangerous short-yardage runs less effective. "Pack" plays were banned; the flying wedge would fly no more.

It took awhile for the changes to have an effect; during the 1909 season, for instance, 33 more players died and injuries continued to mount. But Roosevelt's call for reform had been heard, and the NCAA began to exert control over not just football, but every intercollegiate sport—a control it maintains today.

Other Milestones of 1906

✔ Despite their nickname the "Hitless Wonders," with a team batting average of only .226, the Chicago White Stockings used outstanding pitching in October to defeat their crosstown rivals, the Chicago Cubs, four games to two in the 1906 World Series.

✔ In basketball, the bottoms came off the baskets for the first time; prior to this, play stopped after each successful field goal to remove the ball from the basket. Backboards also came into regular use.

✔ Jay Gould won the first of 18 straight court tennis national titles. Court tennis is a form of the game played on an indoor court. The ball can bounce off the walls and ceiling during play.

✔ In other tennis news, the team from Great Britain won the Davis Cup for the first time, defeating the U.S. team 5–0 at Wimbledon in September.

Olympics . . . Again?

The Olympic movement was reeling from the less-than-spectacular Olympic Games in St. Louis in 1904, and international sportsmen wanted to revive the good feelings created by the first modern Games in 1896. Their solution, in the summer of 1906, was to create a sort of mini-Olympics, which would be held every four years between "regular" Olympics, and always held in Athens, birthplace of the Olympics.

Twenty countries sent a total of 887 athletes to the 1906 Intercalated Games, as they were known, held in July. American athletes, taking part as an official team for the first time, performed well. Charles Daniels (see page 40) won two swimming gold medals, while jumper Ray Ewry continued his success with two more medals. Sprinter Archie Hahn won the 100 meters.

The 1906 Games were considered successful for what they were, with a greater international participation than in 1904. Denmark won the soccer tournament, for instance, while Switzerland's Louis Richardet won six medals in various shooting events.

The good spirits helped revive international interest in the Olympic movement and made planning for the 1908 Games in London (see page 48) more effective. However, in 1910, when the next Intercalated Games were scheduled, Greece was undergoing political upheaval. The Games were cancelled, and the idea of the Intercalated Games was dropped. Today, the 1906 event is not regarded as an "official" Olympic Games.

JOE GANS

42

Among the Best Ever *In 1958, boxing writer Nat Fleischer rated Joe Gans the top lightweight of all time. Tad Dorgan, a veteran boxing writer, called Gans the greatest fighter he ever saw at any weight.*

A Little-Known Champion

Many boxing historians point to a boxing match held on September 3 as one of the greatest—if not the greatest—and most exciting lightweight bouts of all time. The fight was between champion Joe Gans, an African-American fighter who had held the title since 1902, and Battling Nelson, a white challenger.

They squared off in Goldfield, Nevada, for 42 rounds, the longest fight ever held with gloves under the Marquis of Queensbury rules. Gans knocked Nelson down twice, and twice Nelson was "saved by the bell" (he would have been counted out had the round not ended). Nelson's face was cut and he was bleeding from his nose and mouth. Yet he fought on against Gans, described by writers of the time as being a "marvel of speed and science."

Finally, in the 42nd round, Nelson hit Gans with a hard punch. It was an illegal punch, though, aimed well below Gans' waist, and Gans was proclaimed the winner. It was the pinnacle of one of the most successful, yet least well-known, boxing careers. Gans remained the lightweight champion until 1908, when the effects of tuberculosis began to damage his health. His overall record was 120 wins (85 by knockout), 8 losses, and 9 draws.

In 1958, boxing writer Nat Fleischer rated Gans the number-one lightweight of all time. Even as late as 1987, Gans earned a number-three all-time ranking. Tad Dorgan, a veteran boxing writer who covered top fighters in all classes for decades, called Gans the greatest fighter he ever saw, regardless of weight.

1907

Longboat Wins Long Race

The Boston Marathon, first run in 1897, was created after local officials were inspired by the first Olympic marathon in Athens the previous year. Traditionally held in April on Patriots' Day, it was, at first, a mostly small, local affair (it did not top 200 runners until 1928 or 1,000 runners until 1968), but it slowly grew in popularity and size. It was still a far cry from today's event, which attracts more than 20,000 runners. Of course, it is also better organized today. At one point in the April 19, 1907, race, a long freight train crossed the route of the marathon, creating what one newspaper called a "log jam of runners" who had to pause and wait for the train to pass.

The 1907 race was won by a Canadian, a member of the Onandoga Nation named Thomas Longboat. His time of two hours, 24 minutes, and 24 seconds set a record (though his mark would stand for only three years). News reports from the event describe large crowds filling the streets to cheer on the runners—a tradition that still continues.

Although newspapers of the time, reflecting the racial insensitivity of the age, described Longboat with terms such as "the bronze-colored youth," athletic achievement was duly recognized. Two years later (see page TK), marathon running grew massively in popularity, again inspired by an Olympic race.

Surf's Up!

The arrival of Europeans to the islands of Hawaii in the 1600s and 1700s spelled the end for many native traditions. Colonizing settlers, inspired in large part by Christian evangelizing but also by more secular desires for profit, worked hard to "Europeanize" and later to "Americanize" native Hawaiians. One of the oldest practices of the local culture involved riding the ocean waves on wooden boards. Though it nearly died out entirely, a small group of devotees kept the sport and its traditions alive. A pair of events in 1907 helped spread surfing to mainland America and begin its rapid rise to become a key part of world beach culture.

Adventurous Americans visiting what was then the kingdom of Hawaii in the early 1900s tried out the sport, using the long (12 to 16 feet) boards favored by traditionalists. One white native of Hawaii,

Longboat Takes to the Road *Native American runner Tom Longboat (right), shown here at the start of a 1908 race, won the Boston Marathon in 1907 in record time.*

George Freeth, brought his boards to southern California in the summer of 1907. His wave-riding exploits near Redondo Beach were originally a publicity stunt for new railroad line, but they soon caught on. Freeth is regarded today as the father of surfing in America, though many others helped popularize it.

Back in Hawaii, Alexander Ford founded the Outrigger Canoe Club this

1907

The final boost to surfing came from a swimming champion, Duke Kahanamoku (1890–1968). After becoming an international swimming star by winning numerous short- and long-distance races (he won Olympic gold medals in 1912 and 1920), Kahanamoku used his fame to help spread the sport of surfing—a favorite of his from childhood. The attractive, talented, and personable Duke also carried surfing's traditions to Australia, where it became perhaps even more popular than it did in America.

Surfing today is seen as a modern invention, an "extreme" sport most often enjoyed by young people. But its roots extend back before the 20th century . . . dude.

The Doubleday Myth

Who invented baseball? The answer to that question proved to be the beginning of a modern fable that is still believed in some circles today. In 1907, Albert Goodwill Spalding (1850–1915), a former star pitcher turned sporting-goods magnate, was looking for a way to publicize his many baseball products and to assure the public that baseball was an entirely American creation and not the result of years of evolution from earlier, British stick-and-ball games. He appointed the Mills Commission (named for its chairman, National League president A.G. Mills) to look for the true origins and inventor of the "national game." They "discovered" a letter from a man named Abner Graves, claiming that he had witnessed Abner Doubleday organize a game of "base ball" in Cooperstown, New York,

From the Field to a Fortune *Albert Spalding, shown here during his pitching days, became an influential force in sports business after his playing career ended.*

year. One of its goals was to "preserve surfing on boards." The club became one of the islands' largest sports organizations, putting on surfing competitions, offering lessons, and helping legitimize the sport.

in 1839. Doubleday had later gained some fame as a general in the Union Army during the Civil War.

In 1907, Spalding went public with the story, crediting Doubleday with inventing baseball. The announcement generated the publicity—and controversy—that Spalding sought. There was just one problem: It was not true.

Doubleday, as historians even then quickly pointed out, had never been to Cooperstown. He never mentioned baseball in any of his writings. The game Graves described might well have been a form of town ball, which had been played in the United States for nearly a century before 1839. In addition, detailed records from several New York City teams showed their vital influence in codifying baseball's rules, many of which remain nearly unchanged to this day.

Yet so powerful was Spalding, his story was quickly accepted as the truth. Although some experts tried quickly and valiantly to show the errors in the story, it stuck. By 1939, baseball celebrated its "centennial," 100 years after the game that never happened. The site of the Baseball Hall of Fame (the building opened in 1939) was Cooperstown itself, which earned the nickname "Birthplace of Baseball" through sheer mythmaking.

By the 1950s, Doubleday's role in the creation of baseball had been thoroughly and completely discredited by every baseball scholar. However, such is the power of a creation myth such as the one Spalding foisted on the public that Doubleday is sometimes still called the inventor of the game in accounts to this day.

Who was the real "inventor" of the National Pastime? The consensus is that there was not just one creator, but rather several. Most experts point to the 1845 rules laid down by the Knickerbocker Club of New York City, under the leadership of men such as Alexander Cartwright, Daniel Adams, and others, as being the real beginnings of the game we recognize today as baseball. Abner Doubleday had nothing to do with it.

Other Milestones of 1907

✔ John Miskey won the first national squash title. Squash is an indoor game played on an enclosed wooden court using long wooden racquets and a small, hard rubber ball.

✔ Charles W. Oldreive, using specially made long wooden shoes, walked on the Mississippi River from Cincinnati to New Orleans. He covered the 1,600 miles in 40 days, walking only during daylight hours.

✔ The first American balloon race was held on October 21 near St. Louis.

✔ William Learned and Evelyn Sears won the men's and women's U.S. tennis championships, respectively, in September.

✔ In the years before the birth of the National Hockey League (see page 95), the winner of the Stanley Cup as hockey champion was decided by a "challenge" series. That is, a club could challenge the holder of the cup to a series of games. There could be more than one challenge per year. In 1907, this resulted in both the Kenora Thistles (in January) and the Montreal Wanderers (in March) each winning the Stanley Cup.

1908

London Olympics

The Olympics planned for Rome in the summer of 1908 held out hope for the continuation of the Olympic movement, until Mt. Vesuvius erupted in 1906, causing chaos in nearby Rome. The International Olympic Committee turned to London, home of numerous international athletic competitions, to take over. It was an inspired choice. The London Games, held in July, proved to be a model of efficiency, organization, and success that future Games could emulate for decades. In other words, they were everything that Paris (1900) and St. Louis (1904) had not been.

As they had been in the two most recent Olympics, American athletes were central figures. Ray Ewry continued his success in jumping events, adding two more medals to his record total. Mel Sheppard won the 800- and 1,500-meter runs. Americans also played a role in some other significant and bizarre events.

- During the opening ceremonies, teams marched into the stadium under their national flags for the first time. Every nation except the United States dipped its flag when passing the British monarch. The American flag-bearer, shot putter Ralph Rose, said famously afterward, "This flag dips to no earthly king."

- An American won the first marathon run at the current distance of 26 miles, 385 yards. Dorando Pietri of Italy actually finished the race first, but in one of the Olympics' most famous race endings, he was so dazed after he entered the stadium for a final lap that he had to be helped across the line by officials. Unfortunately, that disqualified him, and American Johnny Hayes was later declared the winner. The route had been extended from the planned 25 miles to the new length so that the British royal family could sit in Windsor Castle and see the start of the race.

- A controversy involving American and British runners led to the formation of the first international track organization. During the 400-meter final, a British judge disqualified the apparent winner, American J.C. Carpenter, for interfering with the British runner. A rerun of the race was ordered, but the American refused to take part. Britain's Wyndham Halswelle ran the final by himself. He won.

Jumping for Gold   *With jumps like this one from the 1908 Games, Ray Ewry won a record 10 career gold medals.*

Merkle's Mistake

perhaps the most exciting pennant race in baseball history was decided with the first one-game playoff in baseball history. But what is most remembered about this season is not that playoff game, but a mistake made by one man two weeks earlier.

On September 23, the Chicago Cubs met the New York Giants at the Giants'

home in the Polo Grounds. The two teams were tied for first place in the N.L., and also tied 1–1 heading into the bottom of the ninth inning of this game. The Giants' Moose McCormick was on third base and Fred Merkle was on first. A single by Al Bridwell brought in McCormick, and fans stormed onto the field, assuming the winning run had scored and the game was over. But in the confusion, Merkle did not run to touch second base, instead

1908

heading for the dugout to escape the crowd. Chicago's Johnny Evers realized he could still get Merkle out, and tried to get the ball. If he could touch second before Merkle, the Giants' runner would be out, and the run would not count.

Evers got a ball—no one knows if it was the real game ball—and touched sec-

Tragic Hero *Cleveland pitcher Addie Joss was among the finest players of the era, eventually earning a spot in the Hall of Fame. Sadly, he died of a rare illness only three years after pitching a perfect game.*

ond. With the field awash with people, the umpires ruled the game a tie. Their decision was upheld by the league president. All of this would not have mattered had the teams not finished the regular season tied with identical 98–55–1 records. That meant a one-game playoff was necessary to determine the league champion and the N.L. representative to the World Series. Unfortunately for Merkle, the Giants lost that game 4–2 on October 8, though they had Christy Mathewson pitching for them. Merkle's earlier mistake was seen as the real cause of the Giants' loss, and he was identified with it for the rest of his career.

Joss's Tragic Perfection

In the 20th century, 14 pitchers threw perfect games. Cy Young threw the first (see page 28), and over the next decades other pitchers matched his feat. But none of them did it in the heat of a pennant race.

On October 2, with the A.L. pennant race nearly as tight as that in the N.L., Addie Joss took the mound for the Cleveland Naps (later the Indians). They trailed the Detroit Tigers by a half-game and were a half-game ahead of the Chicago White Sox, whom they played that day. Pitching for Chicago was Ed Walsh, a future Hall of Famer, who later retired with a career earned run average (ERA) of 1.82, the lowest of all time. In second place all-time is Addie Joss, at 1.89. It was truly one of the best pitching matchups ever, and it lived up to its billing.

Walsh finished the day with 15 strikeouts, an A.L. record. He allowed only four

Take Me Out to the Ballgame

The most long-lasting event of the 1908 baseball season came in May, when two men wrote a song that is still sung every day at just about every ballpark in the land. Jack Norworth and Albert Von Tilzer, inspired by a female friend of theirs who loved baseball, wrote "Take Me Out to the Ballgame." It was an instant—and enduring—hit.

Katie Casey was base ball mad.
Had the fever and had it bad;
Just to root for the home town crew,
Ev'ry sou Katie blew.
On a Saturday, her young beau
Called to see if she'd like to go,
To see a show but Miss Kate said,
"No, I'll tell you what you can do."

"Take me out to the ball game,
Take me out with the crowd.
Buy me some peanuts and cracker jack,
I don't care if I never get back,
Let me root, root, root for the home team,
If they don't win it's a shame.
For it's one, two, three strikes, you're out,
At the old ball game."

Katie Casey saw all the games,
Knew the players by their first names;
Told the umpire he was wrong,
All along good and strong.
When the score was just two to two,
Katie Casey knew what to do,
Just to cheer up the boys she knew,
She made the gang sing this song:

"Take me out to the ball game,
Take me out with the crowd.
Buy me some peanuts and cracker jack,
I don't care if I never get back,
Let me root, root, root for the home team,
If they don't win it's a shame.
For it's one, two, three strikes, you're out,
At the old ball game."

hits, and the only run he gave up came on an error by his catcher. Joss literally had to be perfect to win. He was.

Joss threw the second perfect game in modern baseball history (and the last until 1922), winning 1–0. As the final batter was thrown out at first, Cleveland fans rushed the field—and Joss rushed off it. "I am taking no chances," Joss said afterward about fans who had tried to lift him to their shoulders. "Suppose they had let me drop. The season is not done yet."

He was right to be concerned. The Naps failed to win the pennant; Cleveland finished a half-game behind Detroit, although the Tigers had played one fewer game. Later, new rules were put into effect that would not allow that sort of ending to a season.

After a fine 1909 season, Joss suffered through an injury-plagued 1910. In March 1911, on the train back from spring training, he fainted. He returned to his home in Toledo, Ohio to rest, but he faded quickly. At the age of 31, Addie Joss was dead of tubercular meningitis, a disease of the nerves and lungs. The baseball world mourned deeply; a tribute all-star game

1908

featured nine players who would one day be inducted into the Hall of Fame. Joss was also elected to the Hall, but not until 1978 and not until a rule was waived that called for a minimum of 10 years in the major leagues to qualify.

American Car Wins the Day

Far more people in 1908 had seen an auto race than owned automobiles. Racing was still seen as the main use of cars, and the idea of a car in every garage was years away. The dominant cars in most races were made by European automakers such as Mercedes of Germany, Renault of France, and Isotta of Italy. Their machines and drivers came to America and consistently won the top races.

One of the biggest races was the Vanderbilt Cup, held on a racetrack on Long Island, New York. The 1908 race, held on September 3, attracted a large field of top cars and drivers, as well a nearly 250,000 spectators. At the end of the race, the winner was, for the first time, an American driving an American car. George Robertson, driving the No. 16 Locomobile, averaged more than 52 miles per hour and finished nearly two minutes ahead of an Italian car. The victory marked a great leap forward for American car manufacturers and race drivers.

Johnson Versus Burns

America in 1908 was still a very racist nation. African Americans were not welcome in most public situations, let alone in sports. Some places were worse than others, but the overall mood was not welcoming for black people. Into this bubbling cauldron in the first decade of the century came a young African-American boxer from Galveston, Texas, named Jack Johnson (1878–1946).

By early 1908, although he often had trouble arranging fights and battled as much against bigoted crowds as his ring opponents, Johnson was obviously the top contender for the heavyweight title. That title was held by a Canadian fighter named Tommy Burns, who, at only 179 pounds, was one of the smallest heavyweight champs ever. As champ he got to

---

Other Milestones of 1908

✔ The University of Pennsylvania won college football's national championship in December.

✔ During rain delays at baseball games at the Polo Grounds in New York City, canvas tarpaulins were used for the first time to cover the field so that play could resume after the rain passed.

✔ On July 4, Hooks Wiltse of baseball's New York Giants lost his chance for a perfect game by hitting the 27th batter he faced after retiring the previous 26 in a row.

✔ An American team won an around-the-world auto race that ended July 30.

✔ The University of Pittsburgh was the first team to use uniform numbers on its football jerseys.

✔ The first ski jump in the United States was built at Chippewa Falls, Wisconsin.

decide when he would face Johnson to defend the title. Johnson's race played a key role in Burns' decision to avoid him. The records of the time show that Burns and the rest of the boxing world did not want Burns to be the first man to lose the heavyweight title to a black fighter. Making matters worse, in the eyes of Burns' apologists, was Johnson's attitude. He was far from the humble, self-effacing black man that most Americans were used to seeing—people whose spirit had been beaten down by centuries of racism. Johnson had a personality and confidence as powerful as his physique. He expected, and demanded, respect in and out of the ring.

Eventually, Burns traveled to England and other European countries to fight—to fight anyone but Johnson. Johnson followed. Months passed as each man fought a series of lesser bouts. Finally, the boxing match that many people both desired and feared was planned for December 26 in Sydney, Australia.

Famed writer Jack London was among the many who took the long boat ride Down Under to witness the fight. More than 40,000 people filled the arena. Another reason Burns had avoided Johnson soon became apparent: Johnson was the far superior boxer. Though the fight was scheduled for 20 rounds, it was stopped after 14. Johnson had become the first black heavyweight champion in boxing history. "Johnson played with Burns from the gong of the opening round to the finish of the fight," London wrote in the *New York Herald*. The historic result energized Johnson personally, and he took on and defeated a succession of "Great

Historic Fight *Jack Johnson (right) defeated Tommy Burns in this 1908 fight, becoming not only the first black heavyweight champion but a key figure in the history of sports and race in America.*

White Hopes" shamelessly put forward by the boxing establishment to try to take "their" title back from this African-American fighter. They did not succeed until 1915, and even that fight was controversial (see page 82).

Johnson's fights were not all in the ring. For more details on this important American athlete, see page 60.

1909

New Ballparks: Shibe and Forbes

The popularity of baseball filled the coffers of major league owners. Their sole source of income, however, remained ticket sales at their ballparks. While today's teams enjoy revenue from broadcasting, merchandise, parking, and many other sources, teams of the early 1900s were financed almost wholly by their fans.

As the game grew more and more respectable, owners realized that improving the fans' experience at the ballpark would increase attendance and thus revenue. In addition, new engineering techniques were being developed in other areas of construction that meant new ballparks could be constructed of concrete and steel and made larger and more grand than the simple wooden ballparks of the day.

On April 12, Shibe Park opened as the new home of the American League's Philadelphia Athletics. It was a beautiful building, regardless of its purpose. A three-story tower was built into the outside wall at the home plate corner of the building. In the cupola atop this tower was the office of the team's owner, president, and manager, Connie Mack (1862–1956). (A former catcher, Mack began as the Athletics' manager in 1901 and remained at the helm for an incredible 50 years, far and away the longest managerial career in history.) Shibe Park was covered in decorative trim and ringed with glamorous archways. It seated more than 25,000 fans; far more than its predecessor in Philadelphia.

The Athletics paid about $300,000 to build the stadium (perhaps about $3 million in today's dollars, but today's stadiums now cost more than $300 million to build). Shibe Park, unlike its contemporaries, boasted a key feature: parking for 400 cars. The location alongside a row of two-story apartment buildings on 23rd Street meant that enterprising fans could erect small bleachers on their roofs to create a free view of the field. But the most important features of Shibe Park were the materials that made it stand up: concrete and steel, the first such structure in the major leagues.

The innovations continued in Pennsylvania's other big-league city, Pittsburgh (though it was usually spelled without the final "h" in those days). Pirates' owner Barney Dreyfuss built a new ballpark for

Start of a Trend *Philadelphia's Shibe Park marked the beginning of a busy era of stadium construction in the U.S.*

his team and named it for an Army general, John Forbes. Dreyfuss ignored skeptics who believed the location he had chosen for Forbes Field was too far from the city center. He also encouraged the designers to include many "modern" touches in the 25,000-seat ballpark: elevators between levels, dressing rooms for the umpires and visiting teams, an exterior that used color (green and tan), and steel latticework on the outside that called to mind the diamond that lay inside.

The two Pennsylvania ballparks kicked off what would become a building frenzy in baseball. Chicago's Comiskey Park opened in 1910, while Fenway Park in Boston and Tiger Stadium in Detroit opened in 1912. The first game in Wrigley Field (first called Weeghman Park) in Chicago was played in 1913. With these new and splendid palaces to host their paying customers (and revenue sources), baseball owners looked forward to a very prosperous future.

Starting a Run *Johnny Hayes, shown here winning the 1908 Olympic marathon, started a running craze in 1909.*

Hayes' Marathon Inspires New Sports Craze

Though somewhat controversial due to the bizarre ending (see page 48), American Johnny Hayes' victory at the 1908 London Olympics kicked off marathon mania in the United States over the next year. In late 1908 and early 1909, several professional indoor marathons were held, with Italian Dorando Pietri and Hayes among the regular competitors. In fact, Pietri beat Hayes in the first event in November 1908. In February 1909 in St. Louis, Petri lost to Tom Longboat (see page 44). On April 3, a prize of more than $10,000 was offered at an indoor marathon in New York City. Although Pietri, Longboat, and Hayes were all entered, it was Henri St. Yves, a Frenchman running in one of his first marathons, who took home the prize.

Beyond the Eastern professionals, the craze spread West. On May 31, the city of Denver held its first marathon, promoting it as the first such race run at a high altitude (Denver sits about a mile above sea level). Troy Trimble won the race in three hours and 16 minutes, and the *Denver Post* reported that "every man, woman, and child with leisure on their hands went to the great mile track on the outskirts of the city." The runners in this race printed 385 yards into the Overland Park track and then completed 26 one-mile laps.

Some contemporary commentators felt that the real thrill for the many spectators was not the glamour of athletic competition, but more likely a reaction to the struggles of Pietri in 1908. He had fallen five times as he struggled to finish the race, seeming to threaten his health with his exertions. "In order to hold the fickle public's attention, amusement makers must today furnish thrillers in which a good deal of danger is entailed," wrote Lally Collyer in the *Denver Post*. "American people love sport, but they enjoy witnessing dangerous performances better."

Although the Boston Marathon continued strongly, marathons in other cities quickly died out as popularity waned, and the indoor races were not held after 1911.

Across America in a Car

Driving across country today is a relatively simple matter, thanks to interstate highways, fast and reliable cars, and numerous places for travelers to eat and rest on the way. In 1909, however, the way across the nation on wheels was much more treacherous. In 1909, banker Robert Guggenheim offered a $3,500 prize to the winner of the first transcontinental auto race.

Though organizers had hoped for as many as 35 entrants, only six cars actually started out from New York City on June 1. Their destination was Seattle, which was celebrating the Alaska-Yukon-Pacific Exposition; the race's finish would be part of that event.

By the end of the first two days, one car had already dropped out. The way West was not an easy one. There were no paved roads and the cars battled through mud, rain, and snow. As much effort was spent finding a clear and reasonably safe route as was spent doing the actual driving.

The final hurdle for the racers proved to be the Snoqualmie Pass in Washington State. A Model T Ford that had held the lead struck a snow-covered rock atop the pass. When the drivers had to spend seven hours "on the top of the mountain among the clouds," as they later wrote, they were passed by two other cars.

On June 23, another Ford Model T crossed the finish line, but was disqualified because its drivers had changed the car's engine during the race, a violation of the rules. Finishing later that day in Shawmut were Bert W. Scott and C. James Smith, who were declared the official winners. The first cars in the race had completed the journey of more than 3,000 miles in 23 muddy, bumpy, difficult days.

Pittsburgh World Series

Perhaps the two greatest baseball players of their era met in the World Series in October. Ty Cobb (see page 35) led the Detroit Tigers to their third straight A.L. championship, while shortstop Honus Wagner (see the box on page 58) helped the Pittsburgh Pirates to the World Series for the first time since the first Series in

1909

1903 (see page 25). Both players came in as their league's batting champions, Cobb for the third time and Wagner for the seventh. The two men were the best base stealers of the day, as well. Cobb stole only one base in the Series, but it was a key steal of home in the Tigers' game two victory. Wagner ran wild on the Tigers however, stealing six bases, including three in game three as the Pirates won.

Honus Wagner

In 1999, when baseball named its All-Century Team, only one member of that team had begun his career in the 19th century (and only eight had played the bulk of their careers before World War II). In any century, however, Honus Wagner (1874–1955) was one of the finest all-around baseball players of all time. Born John Peter Wagner, he earned his nickname from his German heritage. He started his pro career in 1897 at age 13 with the Louisville Colonels of the National League. In 1900, Louisville's owner, Barney Dreyfuss, traded Wagner and 13 other Colonels to the Pittsburgh Pirates—and then promptly bought that team, as the Colonels were kicked out of the National League.

Wagner played several positions before settling in permanently at shortstop in 1901 at the age of 17. By 1903, he had established himself as a top player, winning the first of his eight N.L. batting titles. In an era when power and extra-base hits were much more rare than today, Wag-

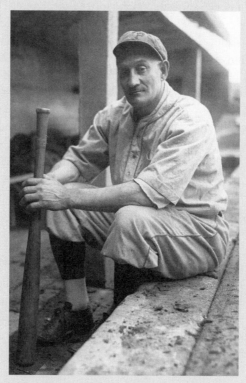

Honus Wagner

ner stood out, leading the league in slugging percentage four times and doubles eight times. He shares a major league record with Babe Ruth and Stan Musial for leading his league in extra-base hits seven times. Wagner became the first player to reach 3,000 hits in his career (though some experts give that credit to 1800s player Cap Anson). His .327 career average is the best ever for a shortstop. On the basepaths, he was equally dangerous, finishing his career with 722 steals, second only to Cobb until 1973.

Wagner's fielding was legendarily excellent. One famous story (probably exaggerated) claims he was so fast with his hands that he once snatched up a rabbit running on the field and threw it to first. His hands were so big that he supposedly threw handfuls of dirt and rocks with every ball.

Wagner, along with Cobb and Babe Ruth, was among the first position players named to the Baseball Hall of Fame in 1936.

Cobb was as angry and difficult as he was skilled, but Wagner combined outstanding baseball skills with a much more relaxed and pleasing manner. "There probably has never been a more genuine, honest, decent, and beloved ballplayer than Honus Wagner," wrote Michael Gershman and Pete Palmer in the *Baseball Biographical Encyclopedia*. The two players were a study in contrasts—the tightly-wound "little ball" of the compact Cobb against the more powerful game of the large Wagner.

During the World Series, the first to go to the full seven games, Wagner was at the top of his game, batting .333 with seven runs batted in (RBI). Cobb struggled, batting only .231 but still leading the Tigers with six RBI. In a Series that featured those two legendary hitters, it was the pitching that made the real difference. Pittsburgh rookie Babe Adams handcuffed Cobb and the Tigers, winning three games and allowing only four earned runs in 27 innings. He blanked Detroit 8–0 in game seven to capture Pittsburgh's first championship.

It was the last time either Cobb or Wagner appeared in the Fall Classic.

Other Milestones of 1909

✔ Football continued to change its rules. Officials voted to change the value of a successful field goal from four points to three points. Other rules changes (see page 41) were still taking effect. The annual game between Army's and Navy's academy teams was cancelled because of continuing public outrage over on-field violence and death.

✔ Yale University won college football's national championship, outscoring its opponents 209–0.

✔ Frank Jackson won the first national horseshoe-pitching championship in Kansas in July.

1910

"Great White Hope"

Jack Johnson scared a lot of people—not just the men who climbed in the ring with him. In 1908 Johnson, an African American, became the world heavyweight boxing champion with a 14th-round knockout of Canadian Tommy Burns in Sydney, Australia (see page 52). Many Americans were not prepared to accept the notion of blacks having equal rights, much less the idea of a physically superior black man.

Johnson, however, was precisely that. As newspapermen eagerly sought out a "Great White Hope" to dethrone the black champ, Johnson mowed down all comers. Finally, former heavyweight champ Jim Jeffries, 35 and now living the life of a farmer, was persuaded to return to the ring against Johnson in a match in Reno, Nevada, on July 4, Independence Day.

The fight's promoter, Tex Rickard, offered Johnson and Jeffries the largest guaranteed purse—$101,000—the sport had ever seen. Rickard promised the winner 60 percent ($60,600) of the money and the loser 40 percent ($40,400).

An audience of 15,760 paid a record $270,775 to watch the epic battle in Reno.

All of Rickard's hype, however, could not disguise the ugliness of the mismatch. With Rickard working the fight as the referee, Johnson toyed with Jeffries before knocking him out in the 15th round.

The outcome of the fight incited rioting across the nation. Nineteen blacks were reportedly killed in the violence.

Johnson's win was a huge blow to the notion of white superiority. It still resounds today as the first great step taken by black athletes in their battle to participate on an equal footing in professional sports in America.

The Law of Batting Averages

Napoleon "Nap" Lajoie of the Cleveland Indians had already won three American League batting titles (in 1901, 1903, and 1904) when the 1910 baseball season began. Ty Cobb of the Detroit Tigers had also won three A.L. batting crowns and was aiming for his fourth straight. Cobb was a fiercely competitive and, among his baseball colleagues, a wildly unpopular player.

The Georgia Peach, as Cobb was known, was batting .383 as the season

SAN FRANCISCO CHRONICLE

CONTESTANTS FOR THE WORLD'S CHAMPIONSHIP, JULY 4, 1910

JAMES J. JEFFRIES

JACK JOHNSON

CHRONICLE HAS THE BEST SPORTING PAGES ON THE PACIFIC COAST

Black and White *This epic July 4 heavyweight bout had as much to do with race relations as it did with boxing.*

neared its end. On October 9, the last day of the regular season, Cobb decided to protect his narrow lead by sitting out the Tigers' game against the Chicago White Sox; he had sat out the previous day's game as well.

Lajoie, the Indians' second baseman, played both games of a doubleheader against the St. Louis Browns. Jack O'Connor, the manager of the Browns, ordered his rookie third baseman, John "Red" Corriden, to play almost on the edge of the outfield grass when Lajoie batted. Lajoie took advantage of the Browns' gift. In the first game he had four hits in four at-bats, with one triple and three bunt singles. In the second game he had four more bunt singles. At day's end Lajoie had eight hits in nine at-bats (he reached base a ninth time on an error) and it appeared as if he had bunted his way past Cobb with a .384 average. Eight of Cobb's own teammates reportedly sent Lajoie messages of congratulations.

American League president Ban Johnson was furious, suspecting the Browns had conspired to give Lajoie the batting title by ordering Corriden to play

A Tradition Begins

On April 14, William Howard Taft, the 27th president of the United States, became the first person to throw out the ceremonial first pitch of a new baseball season. Taft tossed the ball to Washington Senators pitcher Walter Johnson, who then pitched a one-hitter in a 3–0 victory against the Philadelphia Athletics.

so deep in the field. Johnson recalculated the final averages and announced that Cobb's was .384944, while Lajoie's was .384084. Cobb won. The Chalmers Automobile Company, which had promised to award a car to the A.L. batting champion, gave cars to both players.

Cobb, despite the best efforts of Lajoie and the St. Louis Browns, won his fourth straight batting title. He eventually wound up leading the American League in hitting for nine consecutive years.

In 1981, 20 years after Cobb's death, *The Sporting News* revisited the 1910 batting race. The magazine found that in computing Cobb's average, the feisty centerfielder was credited twice for one game in which he had two hits. By correcting that error, Cobb's average fell below Lajoie's. The commissioner's committee, however, voted unanimously to leave the record books alone. Cobb remains the recognized 1910 A.L. batting champ.

Athletics Win World Series

The Chicago Cubs won 104 games and their fourth National League pennant in five seasons. In fact, the Cubs ran away with the pennant by 13 games. Although their opponent in the 1910 World Series, the Philadelphia Athletics, won 102 games, the Cubs were favored because, after all, they had already won two of the first six World Series.

However, the American League season ended a week earlier than the National League's. While the Cubs were playing meaningless games, the Athletics tuned up by playing five games against an A.L. All-Star team that featured future Hall of Famers Ty Cobb, Tris Speaker, Walter Johnson, and Ed Walsh.

The Athletics entered the World Series in October with only two starting pitchers, but both were aces. Charles "Chief" Bender, so-called because his mother was a Chippewa Indian, had a 23–5 record. Teammate Jack Coombs was even more impressive. The 27-year-old pitched 13 shutouts, including a then-record 53 consecutive scoreless innings, while compiling a 31–9 record.

Bender started and finished game one, allowing three hits in a 4–1 win at Shibe Park in Philadelphia. Coombs was not as masterful the next day, but the Athletics won again, 9–3. Two days later in Chicago, Coombs pitched his second complete-game victory in a 12–5 romp. His three hits and three RBI staked the Athletics to a commanding 3–0 Series lead.

The Chief pitched for the Athletics in game four. A sweep seemed inevitable when Bender strode to the mound with a 3–2 lead in the bottom of the ninth inning. But Cubs player-manager Frank Chance tripled, sending home Frank "Wildfire" Schulte to tie the score, and the Cubs won it one inning later.

It was too little, too late for the Cubs. The following day Coombs scattered nine hits in a Series-clinching 7–2 victory. The A's had won their first world title and in the process used only two pitchers, Bender and Coombs, to work all 46 innings.

A Famous Poem

As the Chicago Cubs roared to another National League pennant in 1910, New York *Daily Mail* writer Franklin Adams wrote a short bit of doggerel that remains among the most famous baseball writings ever, and probably played a big part in three players earning places in the Baseball Hall of Fame.

Writing in 1910, Adams described the double-play exploits of Cubs infielders Joe Tinker, Johnny Evers, and Frank Chance. Though they were far from the best infielders of their day and, in fact, their double-play totals were not that great, the fame they earned from the poem propelled them firmly into baseball lore. All three were elected to the Hall of Fame, though individually none of them probably deserved it. (A gonfalon, by the way, is an archaic nickname for a pennant, which the Cubs won over Adams' favored New York Giants).

These are the saddest of possible words,
Tinker to Evers to Chance.
Trio of Bear Cubs and fleeter than birds,
Tinker to Evers to Chance.
Thoughtlessly pricking our gonfalon
    bubble,
Making a Giant hit into a double,
Words that are weighty with nothing but
    trouble,
Tinker to Evers to Chance.

Other Milestones of 1910

✔ Speed demon Barney Oldfield, driving a Benz auto across a one-mile course in Daytona Beach, Florida, set a new land speed record of 131.77 miles per hour on March 16.

✔ On October 15, middleweight boxer Stanley Ketchel, known as "The Michigan Assassin," was shot and killed by Walter Dipley, a jealous husband. Ketchel, only 24, died with a lifetime record of 53–4–4 (50 of his wins were by knockout) and is considered one of the all-time great middleweights.

✔ Harvard University's football team outscored its opponents 155–5 to finish the season with a record of 8–0–1. The Harvard Crimson ended the season with a 0–0 tie against archrival Yale University on November 19 and was named national champion by the Helms Athletic Foundation.

1911

The First Indy 500

On May 30, the first International 500 Mile Sweepstakes (known today as the Indianapolis 500) was held at the five-year-old Indianapolis Motor Speedway. Forty-four drivers entered in hopes of claiming the $10,000 first prize.

While the 2.5-mile rectangular track was the same length as the one used today, much else about the race was different. For instance, each car contained two men: a driver and an on-board "mechanician," whose primary job was to keep an eye out for cars coming from behind. Top speeds were well below 100 m.p.h., and because the race lasted about seven hours, drivers were allowed to use a relief driver for small portions of the race.

Of the drivers entered, only Ray Harroun, a 29-year-old engineer for the Indianapolis-based Marmon Automobile Company, chose not to use a mechanician. Harroun did not want his yellow six-cylinder Marmon Wasp with the maroon number 32 to carry what he believed to be the excessive and unnecessary weight of two people. Harroun's competitors complained that without an on-board lookout, he would be a safety hazard.

Harroun responded by using his engineer's ingenuity. He bolted a small mirror to the front of his cockpit, and the first automobile rearview mirror was born.

The first Indy 500 was only 12 laps into the race when it had its first fatality. A front tire flew off Arthur Greiner's Amplex, sending the vehicle hopping around the track. Greiner's mechanician, S.P. Dickson, was pitched against a fence and killed immediately.

Meanwhile, Harroun and his relief driver, Cy Patschke, took advantage of their car's lighter weight. The Marmon Wasp, with Harroun at the wheel, crossed the finish line in the winning time of 6 hours, 42 minutes, 8 seconds. Its average speed was 74.6 miles per hour.

Stunt Flying

It may be that stunt flying was more a fad than an actual sport, but it certainly held the public's fascination this year. In fact, 1911 was ushered in with two bizarre stunt flying incidents, both of them involving fatalities. On New Year's Eve, 1910, aviator Archibald Hoxsey attempted to better his own world-record altitude mark of 11,474 feet in the skies

First Speed King *An American racing tradition began when Ray Harroun drove to victory in the first Indy 500.*

over Los Angeles. He encountered turbulence, however, and his plane plunged to the earth, killing him. That same day in New Orleans John B. Moisant, flying a Bleriot monoplane, crashed while trying to set a new endurance-flying record.

Aviators were folk heroes in 1911. Harriet Quimby, an attractive and daring New Yorker, became the first woman to become a licensed pilot this year. And on September 5 she made a moonlight flight over Staten Island as 20,000 spectators watched the first woman to make a night flight. Quimby was more renowned for her stylish outfits than her aviation prowess. She died in a crash in 1913.

The ace of aviation was Lincoln "The Birdman" Beachey. Beachey earned $1,000 a week—a huge sum—performing death-defying aerial stunts. His most spectacular feat occurred on June 27, when he flew into Niagara Falls and then barely scaled the gorge downstream.

Four years later Beachey died in the air. While performing his signature "dive of death" above San Francisco Bay on March 14, 1915, Beachey was betrayed by his airplane. The force of the 3,000-foot plunge tore the wings from his plane. Beachey disappeared into the frigid waters of the bay, another casualty of the public's fascination with flight.

In Her Flying Machine *New Yorker Harriet Quimby became the first woman to earn a pilot's license. Americans were fascinated with airplanes and stunt flying in 1911 (see page 64).*

A Miss and a Victory

The Philadelphia Athletics, with their so-called "$100,000 Infield" of Frank Baker, Jack Barry, Eddie Collins, and Stuffy McInnis, cruised to the 1911 American League pennant by 13 1/2 games, then beat the N.L's New York Giants in six games in the World Series.

This was the Series in which Baker, the Athletics' third baseman, earned the nickname "Home Run" Baker. After the Giants won the opener 2–1 behind Christy Mathewson's pitching, Baker belted a game-winning home run in game two. In game three, with one out in the ninth inning and New York leading 1-0, Baker walloped a game-tying homer off Mathewson. The A's won in the 11th inning.

Then it rained as if Noah were building an ark. For six days it poured, so Game 4 was played one week after game three. The Giants again sent Mathewson to the mound—his third start in four games. The A's got the better of Mathewson, 4–2, to take a 3–1 Series lead.

Game 5 featured the most memorable play of this Series. With the score tied 3–3 with one out in the 10th inning at the Polo Grounds, the Giants had the potential winning run on third base. Fred Merkle hit a long fly ball in foul territory. A's rightfielder Danny Murphy might have been wise not to catch it, but he did. The Giants' runner on third, Larry Doyle, tagged the base and then headed for home—and beat Murphy's throw to the plate. The Giants won. Or had they?

Doyle's slide missed home plate by at least six inches. The A's catcher never tagged the runner, though. Home plate umpire Bill Klem waited for the A's to lodge a protest, but the infield was already jammed with jubilant fans. Later, Athletics manager Connie Mack said he felt it would have been unsportsmanlike to protest the play.

The Giants won the game, 4–3, but one day later at Philadelphia's Shibe Park the Athletics exacted revenge. Philadelphia's seven-run seventh inning buried the Giants. The Athletics won the game, 13–2, and their second World Series in as many years.

11/11/11: College Football's Big Day

On November 4, unbeaten Princeton University met the defending national champion Harvard Crimson in the most anticipated college football game of the season. Princeton eked by Harvard, 8–6. The following Saturday, though, provided two much more memorable games. The Princeton Tigers played Dartmouth College who, like Princeton, entered the November 11 game unbeaten.

Harvard, meanwhile, was hosting the Carlisle Indian School. Carlisle was not regarded as a threat, despite its 8–0 record. Carlisle had the great Jim Thorpe (1888–1953), who punted, kicked, and starred as a halfback and on defense.

Thorpe, nursing sore legs, had suited up but was not supposed to play. Once the Crimson took an early lead, however, the great halfback ambled onto the field. In an amazing performance, Thorpe kicked four field goals and one extra point. His 48-yard-field goal was the margin of victory as Carlisle won, 18–15.

Princeton, meanwhile, had its hands full with Dartmouth before 10,000 spectators. Late in the fourth quarter of a 0–0 game, Princeton's Hobey Baker pounced on a fumble at Dartmouth's 35-yard line. After two plays (in 1911 a team had only three downs to advance the ball 10 yards, not four), the Tigers decided to attempt a 45-yard field goal. What followed was one of the more bizarre plays ever.

The Princeton kicker kicked a low line drive. Nearing the crossbar, the football hit a Dartmouth player on the back, ricocheted skyward, hit the ground, and then, amazingly, bounced through the uprights. The referee, after consulting his rule book for more than five minutes, signaled that the kick was good. The rule book said nothing about the ball hitting an opposing player or the ground. It stated only that if the ball passed between the goal posts, the kick was good.

Princeton won 3–0. A week later the Tigers defeated Yale to finish 8–0–2 and win the national championship.

Other Milestones of 1911

✔ Clarence DeMar, clocked in a time of 2:21.39, won the first of his record-seven Boston Marathons on April 19.

✔ J.P. Jones of Cornell University ran a world-record 4:15.4 mile on May 27 at the IC4A national college championships at Soldiers Field in Cambridge, Mass.

✔ New York governor Charles Evans Hughes outlawed all betting at racetracks across the state. Horseracing suffered dearly under the two-year ban.

✔ John McDermott, 21, of Atlantic City, N.J., became the first American-born golfer to win the U.S. Open, which for 16 years had been won only by British golfers, on June 26 at the Chicago Golf Club.

✔ In tennis, William Larned of Summit, New Jersey, won his fifth consecutive U.S. Open on September 3, defeating Maurice McLoughlin of San Francisco in straight sets at age 38. Larned, the premier male player of the early century, won seven U.S. titles between 1901 and '11. A day earlier, on the ladies' side, Hazel Hotchkiss won her third consecutive U.S. Open.

1912

Introducing Pinstripes and Fenway Park

The 1912 season saw the debut of two beloved baseball icons: pinstripes and Fenway Park. The New York Yankees are famous for wearing pinstripes on their home uniforms. The Boston Red Sox, who are the Yankees' archrivals (theirs is perhaps the greatest rivalry in baseball), are renowned for their unique and charming home field, Fenway Park.

Before 1912, however, neither pinstripes nor Fenway Park existed. In fact, the Yankees were known as the Highlanders and did not change their name until 1913.

The Red Sox were scheduled to open Fenway Park, so named because it was built in the Fenway section of Boston, on April 18. The opponent? The New York Highlanders. Six days earlier, on April 12, the Highlanders made a fashion statement by donning the now-famous pinstripes for the first time on their home uniforms.

The Fenway Park grand opening was overshadowed by tragedy and delayed by rain. On April 15, three days before the scheduled opener, the new ocean liner *Titanic* sank in the Atlantic Ocean. More than 1,500 people died. Understandably, the catastrophe was front-page news for days and days.

On April 18 the scheduled opener was rained out. The rain continued on April 19. Finally, on Saturday, April 20, Fenway Park hosted its first Major League Baseball game. Some 27,000 fans were in attendance.

The Highlanders entered the game with a five-game losing streak. New York scored three runs in the top of the first inning off Red Sox spitball ace (the spitball was a legal pitch at the time) Buck O'Brien. The Sox rallied to tie the score, however. The game went into extra innings with the score tied at 6–6. In the bottom of the 11th inning, Boston center fielder Tris Speaker ended the 3-hour, 20-minute marathon with an RBI single. Boston won 7–6.

Today, Fenway Park is the oldest ballpark in Major League Baseball. Although the stadium still looks much as it did on April 20, 1912, it is worth noting that the fabled Green Monster—the 37-foot high left-field wall—was not built until 1934. Before then, left field ended with a steep

World's Greatest Athlete *Jim Thorpe won the pentathlon and the decathlon at the 1912 Olympics (see page 70).*

10-foot embankment where fans sat. That ridge was known as "Duffy's Cliff" after Red Sox leftfielder Duffy Lewis.

A Classic Finish at Indy

At the Indianapolis 500 auto race on May 30, Ralph DePalma set a new standard for the sports ideal of never giving up. DePalma was leading the race by 10 miles over his closest competitor, Joe Dawson, with just five laps (12 1/2 miles) remaining. Suddenly, DePalma's Mercedes began leaking oil and the engine started sputtering. DePalma was faced with a dilemma. The safe strategy would have been to make a pit stop in hopes of fixing the problem and perhaps salvaging a top five finish. Instead, DePalma made the risky decision to go for it.

The Longest Mile *Ralph DePalma completed 499 miles of the Indianapolis 500 before his car gave out. DePalma got out and pushed, but was disqualified from the race.*

With less than one mile to go, however, his broken-down car stopped working. DePalma and his riding partner, the mechanic Rupert Jeffkins, got out of the car and pushed the 2,500-pound automobile toward the pits as Joe Dawson blew by them for the easy victory. Although DePalma was disqualified, his courageous effort was captured in a famous newspaper photograph that did much to glorify the new race in the eyes of the American public.

The Stockholm Olympics

The Swedes staged an Olympics in July that was a resounding success. There was international goodwill as a then-record 28 nations took part. Innovations such as electronic timing and a public-address system were introduced.

The United States set the pace with 25 gold medals, including the two won by Jim Thorpe (see below). Among the other American highlights in Stockholm:

- Brothers Platt and Ben Adams competed in the final of the standing high jump. Platt bettered his brother with a leap of 5 feet, 4 inches.

- Ralph Craig sprinted to gold medals in both the 100- and 200-meter races. The 100-meter race had seven false starts before Craig rallied in the closing strides of the eighth start.

- Americans finished 1–2–3 in the 800-meter run as each man broke the existing world record. James "Ted" Meredith, a lightly regarded 19-year-old, earned the gold in a race in which the top five finishers were separated by no more than four meters.

- In swimming, colorful Hawaiian Duke Kahanamoku cruised to victory in the 100-meter freestyle. So convincing was the Duke's win that on the last lap he turned around to see where his nearest competitor was. Eyeing no threat, Kahanamoku coasted home effortlessly.

In the Greco-Roman wrestling final match, two light heavyweights, Sweden's Anders Ahlgren and Finland's Ivar Bohing, wrestled nine hours with neither man giving in. Finally a draw was declared, and the two were awarded silver medals.

Jim Thorpe's Monster Year

Few athletes have ever accomplished more than Jim Thorpe did in 1912. As the dominant track and field athlete of his era, the Sac-and-Fox Indian won two gold medals at the Olympics in Stockholm, Sweden in July. And as the nation's most dominant college football player, Thorpe scored 198 points and led tiny Carlisle (Pennsylvania) Indian School to a 12–1 record.

Thorpe's first fabulous feat of 1912 occurred on May 25. Carlisle was competing against unbeaten Lafayette College in a dual track meet. Legend has it that Thorpe arrived at the meet accompanied by one other schoolmate.

"You mean the two of you are the whole team?" asked a Lafayette official.

"Nope," Thorpe was said to have replied. "Just me. The other fellow's the student manager."

In truth, the 6-foot, 190-pound Thorpe was one of six members of the Carlisle track team. Still, that day Thorpe won six of the seven events he entered. Carlisle easily won the meet, 71–41.

Two months later Thorpe was in Stockholm for the Olympics. He was en-tered in two of the most grueling track and field events, the pentathlon and the decathlon. The pentathlon combines five events and the decathlon 10. Thorpe was really competing in 15 events, then, in his quest to win two gold medals.

He did. Easily.

In the pentathlon Thorpe won four of the five events: the broad jump, discus throw, 200-meter dash, and 1,500-meter run. He placed third in the javelin throw.

The decathlon followed. Thorpe defeated all rivals in four events. He did well enough in the other six events to win his second gold medal of the Games.

The Swedish king, Gustav V, was deeply impressed. "Sir," the monarch told Thorpe upon meeting him, "you are the greatest athlete in the world."

Thorpe was not yet done. On November 9, Thorpe and his Carlisle football teammates met West Point with a 9–0–1 record. Still, Carlisle was considered an underdog to the mighty Army squad.

Sounds More Familiar

The reforms in college football begun in 1906 (see page 41) continued throughout the years before World War I.

In 1912, three important rules were instituted that today's fans will find familiar.

Fields were standardized as being 100 yards long, with 10-yard deep end zones. Prior to this, fields were larger or smaller depending on what a school had available for space. Also, a touchdown's worth was increased from five points to six (an extra point was worth one point). And a team was now given four downs (instead of three) to advance the ball 10 yards and make a first down.

These changes, plus the growing influence of the forward pass, helped football get ready for a leap in popularity with the coming of superstar running back Red Grange and the birth of the National Football League in 1920.

1912

Once again, though, Thorpe was dominant. He scored two touchdowns (each touchdown was five points), passed for a third, and kicked three field goals and three extra points in Carlisle's 27–6 whupping of Army. In other words, Thorpe had a hand—or a foot—in every point his team scored that day.

The afternoon's most memorable sequence occurred when Thorpe fielded an Army kick on his own 10-yard line and returned it 90 yards for a touchdown. The play was nullified by a penalty. Army kicked again. This time Thorpe fielded the ball on his own five-yard line—and returned it 95 yards for a touchdown.

Thorpe was a punishing running back. One member of the Army defense was so banged up from his fruitless efforts to tackle Thorpe on this afternoon that he never played football again. That cadet was future five-star general and the 34th President of the United States, Dwight Eisenhower.

The Baseball Rematch

The 1912 World Series in October was a rematch of an earlier Series that had never been played. If that sounds strange, consider this: It was also the first best-of-seven series that lasted eight games!

The Boston Red Sox and the New York Giants were supposed to have met in the second World Series in 1904. Giants manager John McGraw thumbed his nose at the upstart American League and its representative, however, and declined to play the Sox. The 1904 World Series was never played (see page 32).

The Giants had a pair of future Hall of Fame pitchers in Christy Mathewson and Rube Marquard. Mathewson won 23

Other Milestones of 1912

Eddie Collins

✔ On September 11, Philadelphia Athletics second baseman Eddie Collins stole a Major League Baseball-record six bases against the Detroit Tigers. Eleven days later Collins repeated the feat, swiping six bases against the St. Louis Browns.

✔ The Quebec Bulldogs won hockey's Stanley Cup in March in the first season in which each team skated with six men on each team (previously, they played seven to a side).

✔ Ty Cobb became the first Major Leaguer Baseball player to bat above .400 in consecutive seasons as he won his sixth consecutive batting title.

✔ Harvard went undefeated (9–0) in college football and was named national champion.

games that season and Marquard 26. Marquard established a modern record by opening 1912 with 19 consecutive wins.

Boston countered with 22-year-old star "Smokey" Joe Wood, who had a 34–5 record. Wood won three more games in this Series. The Red Sox also won 105 games in 1912, which remains a team record.

Game two of the Series finished in a 6–6 tie at Fenway Park in Boston. The Giants led 6–5 in the bottom of the 10th inning when Red Sox center fielder Tris Speaker circled the bases with an inside-the-park home run, tyin the score at six apiece. After another scoreless inning, the game was called due to darkness. The game was declared a tie.

From there the fortunes of the Series see-sawed. Boston went up 3–1. New York stormed back to tie the Series at 3–3.

Finally, on October 16 at Fenway Park, the Giants and Red Sox met in the decisive game 8. New York took a 2–1 lead in the top of the 10th inning off Wood. A world championship was three outs away.

The bottom of the 10th was, for New York, a tragedy of errors. Centerfielder Fred Snodgrass dropped lead-off hitter Clyde Engle's routine fly pop-up. After Snodgrass made a great catch on the next batter, Speaker hit a lame foul pop fly between the Giants first baseman and catcher that neither player bothered to catch.

Given a second chance, Speaker singled off Mathewson to bring in Engle with the tying run. Two batters later, Red Sox third baseman Larry Gardner hit the game-winning—and Series winning—sacrifice fly.

The 3–2 10th-inning win capped a milestone season for Boston. The Red Sox had moved into brand-new Fenway Park (see page 68) and then won the final game of the Series in it.

1913

Upset Special at the U.S. Open

When the U.S. Open golf tournament began in September at The Country Club in Brookline, Massachusetts, most observers expected the champion would come from across the Atlantic Ocean. Nobody thought the winner would literally be the boy next door. British golfers Harry Vardon and Ted Ray, both professionals, were the sport's elite, and it was expected that one of them would win. Few people were surprised when, after three rounds, they were tied for the lead.

However, there was a third player, an unknown amateur, also atop the leader board. His name was Francis Ouimet. He was 20 years old and he had grown up across the street from the golf course on which he was now playing. Ouimet, in fact, had been a caddy on the course, earning 28 cents a round.

During the fourth round of play, Ouimet, accompanied by his 10-year-old caddy, Eddie Lowery, fell behind early. Two birdies (one shot under par) on the second nine holes salvaged his round, and put him into a three-way playoff with Ray and Vardon the following day.

By September 20, a Monday, news of Ouimet's upset bid had spread throughout nearby Boston. The Brookline course was lined with new fans of the sport. While Ray and Vardon, the seasoned pros, wilted, Ouimet and Lowery (who missed school to caddy on this day) played as if they had not a care in the world.

Vardon shot a 77 on the 18-hole playoff. Ray shot a 78. Ouimet, meanwhile, shot a 72. The boy next door had pulled off the biggest upset in the history of golf, and, in the process, given it mass appeal on this side of the Atlantic.

The Big Train

If you were to name a Cy Young Award winner for the decade—other than Cy Young himself, who retired in 1911—it would undoubtedly be Walter Johnson of the Washington Senators.

Johnson, also known as "The Big Train," won more games (264) and struck out more batters (2,219) during the 1910s than anyone else. Only in 1911 did the long-armed, right-hander fail to lead the American League in strikeouts. His best year may have been 1913, though, when he won 36 games and lost only seven.

Fresh-Faced Kid *American Francis Ouimet (center) was just 20 years old when he stunned elite British golfers Harry Vardon (left) and Ted Ray (right) to win the U.S. Open.*

It was a monster season for Johnson, who led the majors in every notable pitching category. He was tops in wins, shutouts (11), strikeouts (243), and complete games (29), had the lowest ERA (1.09), and was named the American League's Most Valuable Player. His streak of 55 scoreless innings that year stood as a big-league record for 55 years, and no pitcher since has won as many games in one season.

Thorpe Stripped of His Medals

In the early part of the century, it was not uncommon for a college athlete to earn extra money by playing semi-professional sports in the off season. It was against the rules, but not uncommon. Jim Thorpe, for example, spent the summers of 1909 and 1910 playing Minor League

1913

Big Train *Washington's Walter Johnson had one of the greatest seasons by a pitcher in big-league history (see page 74).*

selecting athletes to represent the United States in the Olympics, demanded an explanation.

"I never realized what a big mistake I made by keeping a secret about my ball playing and I am sorry I did so," Thorpe wrote in a letter to the A.A.U. "I hope I will be partly excused by the fact that I was simply an Indian schoolboy and did not know all about such things."

The A.A.U. took no pity on Thorpe. The greatest athlete in the world was stripped of both the gold medals he earned at the previous summer's Olympics in Stockholm (see page 70). He immediately signed a baseball contract with the New York Giants, but he was never the same person.

Despite numerous pleas by Thorpe, his family, and his many admirers around the world, his medals were never returned to him during his lifetime. Only in 1983, 30 years after Thorpe died destitute and alone, did the International Olympic Committee return his medals to his family.

Baseball for a team in North Carolina. He earned $25 per week doing so. Unlike many of his peers—college athletes who moonlighted as pro baseball players—Thorpe used his real name on the baseball roster. (Most players did not so they would not be caught breaking the rules.)

In January of 1913 a sportswriter happened upon a team photo of Thorpe's Winston-Salem, North Carolina, squad and recognized the Olympic and college football legend's name. The story spread like wildfire. The Amateur Athletic Union (A.A.U.), which was responsible for

Notre Dame 35, Army 13

The forward pass had been a legal offensive tool in college football since 1906. However, most teams only considered passing the ball as a last resort. Notre Dame University, like the forward pass, entered the 1913 season as an afterthought. The small Midwest Catholic university had compiled an impressive 38–2–5 record since 1907, but the Fighting Irish of Notre Dame had never traveled east. The powerhouse teams—Yale, Harvard, Princeton and Army—were all in the East.

On November 1, Notre Dame traveled to West Point in New York State to play Army. The Irish had won their first three games by a combined score of 169–7, but that had come against vastly inferior competition than the West Point Cadets, who had won their first four games by a combined 72–6 score.

Notre Dame had a secret weapon, though. During the previous summer quarterback Gus Dorais and end Knute Rockne had worked together as lifeguards at Cedar Point, Ohio. The two pals had worked on passing a football, which at the time was a novelty.

When the game began, with 5,000 curious fans in attendance, Notre Dame opened up its aerial attack immediately. Dorais' first two passes fell incomplete, but during the rest of the afternoon the All-American quarterback was nearly perfect.

Dorais completed 14 of his next 15 passes as the Irish stunned the Cadets 35–13. Dorais' numbers, all unheard of passing figures at the time, were 14–17 for 243 yards and three touchdowns. Dorais' longest completion, a 40-yard pass to Rockne, was the longest pass play anyone had ever seen.

Rockne, the future legendary coach, was a wily athlete and innovator. Just before catching the game's first touchdown pass, a 25-yarder, he had limped onto the field. Then, when the play started, Rockne sprinted past Army's defenders to haul in Dorais' throw.

The afternoon was revolutionary. Never before had a wide receiver and a quarterback attempted a timing pattern. Previously, wide receivers just ran to a spot and wait for the pass. Rockne and Dorais figured out how to calculate when a runner would be at a certain position on the field, so the quarterback could throw the football to that spot and the receiver could catch it without having to break his stride.

After Notre Dame's rout of Army, college football, and the Fighting Irish's humble place in it, would never be the same.

Other Milestones of 1913

✔ On March 10, the Quebec Bulldogs swept two games from the Sydney Millionaires to win hockey's Stanley Cup.

✔ On May 6 the Federal League, an alternative professional baseball league with seven teams, quietly made its debut. It would last for only two seasons.

✔ The longest long shot ever won the Kentucky Derby. On May 10, Donerail, a 91-to-1 long shot, won the Kentucky Derby, paying $184.90 for a $2 bet.

✔ On May 30, French driver Jules Goux won the Indy 500. Goux took the checkered flag 13 minutes in front of runner-up Spencer Wishart, which is still a record as the largest margin of victory ever at the Indy 500.

✔ Former major league ballplayer-turned-evangelist Billy Sunday attracted nearly 700,000 attendees to 94 services he preached at this year. The aptly named preacher later tried to outlaw Sunday baseball.

✔ On December 19, heavyweight boxing champion Jack Johnson retained his title after fighting to a 10-round draw against Jim Johnson in Paris, France.

1914

A Major Alternative

The Federal League, baseball's third "major" league after the American and National Leagues, actually began play in 1913. In that year, however, the Federal League made no pretensions to challenging the other leagues' dominance. The 1913 edition of the Federal League included six Midwestern teams playing a six-week schedule with no former major league players—except as managers. Cy Young, for example, managed the Cleveland team.

In 1914, though, the Federal League expanded to eight teams and into eastern U.S. cities such as Baltimore and Buffalo. And it began tempting Major League Baseball players to jump to the new league. On April 13—one day before Major League Baseball's opening day—the Federal League launched its season as the Baltimore Terrapins beat the Buffalo Feds 3–2 in front of 27,140 spectators. The American and National Leagues took notice.

Shortstop Joe Tinker and pitcher Mordecai "Three Finger" Brown, both future members of the National Baseball Hall of Fame, soon signed with the upstart league. Superstar pitcher Walter Johnson nearly signed with the league, too, but at the last moment the American League chipped in to pay for The Big Train's salary increase.

The Federal League, hounded by lawsuits from the other two leagues, soon began losing money. Fans, their curiosity satisfied, returned to watching the American and National League teams. Two desperate franchises, the Brooklyn Tip Tops and the Pittsburgh Filipinos, reduced ticket prices from 50 cents to a quarter.

Meanwhile, a few players did shine. Indianapolis Hoosier Benny Kauff, a rookie, led the league in batting with a .370 average. Former Pittsburgh Pirates pitcher Claude Hendrix went 29–11 for the Chicago Whales. The Hoosiers, led by Kauff and four other .300 hitters, won the pennant by half a game over the Whales.

A year later the Federal League folded. In exchange for its surrender, Federal League owners were paid $600,000—an enormous sum in those days—by the American and National Leagues. Meanwhile, the American and National Leagues were the first professional leagues—though certainly not the last—to successfully eliminate an upstart rival.

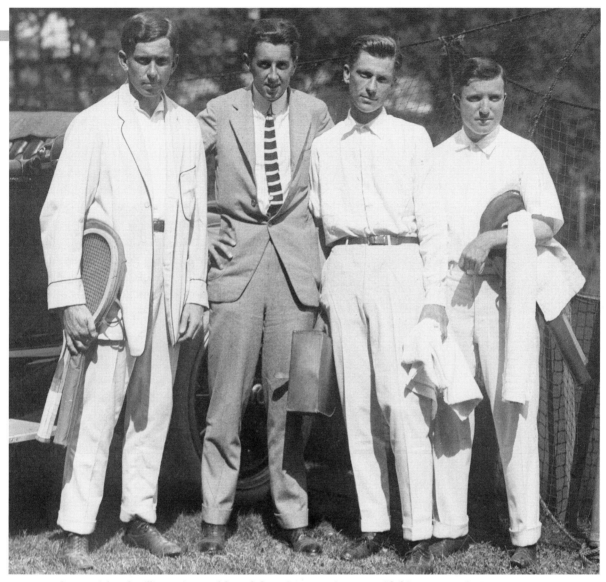

True Survivor *Richard Williams (second from left; see page 81) poses with his 1914 Davis Cup teammates.*

The Miracle Braves

On July 19 , baseball's Boston Braves began the afternoon in Cincinnati and in the National League cellar. The last-place team had a 33–43 record and trailed the first-place New York Giants by 15 1/2 games.

That afternoon, though, Boston swept a doubleheader from the Cincinnati Reds. Afterward, Braves manager George Stallings (who had one rule for his rowdy players—"Do what you want but don't wind up in jail and come to play every day") told them, "Now we'll catch New York."

Miracle Worker *Shortstop Rabbit Maranville played a key role for Boston's "Miracle" Braves of 1914. Maranville eventually played 23 big-league seasons and was elected to the Hall of Fame in 1954.*

When Braves pitcher Dick Rudolph, a former Giant, warned his ex-teammates of Boston's ambition, they yawned. "You're wasting your time," they said.

By August 10, just a little more than three weeks later, the Braves had won nine games in a row and climbed six spots, from last place to second. Led by pitchers Rudolph and Bill James, each of whom won 26 games for the season, Boston found itself 6 1/2 games behind the Giants.

Rudolph and James were not the only Braves performing miracles. Pitcher Lefty Tyler put together a 23-inning scoreless streak in August. Pitcher George "Iron" Davis, a Harvard law student, pitched a no-hitter. Zany shortstop Walter "Rabbit"

Maranville, who once jumped into a hotel lobby fish tank, leaned into a bases-loaded pitch—with his forehead—to force in the game-winning run in a 1–0 win at Pittsburgh. (Any batter hit by a pitch automatically goes to first base.)

By now the Braves had won over their hometown to the extent that Boston Red Sox owner Joe Lannin offered them the use of his newer and more spacious Fenway Park. The Braves moved out of their home field, the South End Grounds, for the remainder of the season.

On September 8, Boston beat the Giants, 8–3, at Fenway to take sole possession of first place. After that, the Braves went 25–6 while manager John McGraw's Giants, the N.L. representative in the past three World Series, went 16–16. The Miracle Braves, 15 1/2 games out in July, won the pennant by 10 1/2 games.

The Braves had one more miracle remaining. Four, actually. Facing the mighty Philadelphia Athletics, winners of three of the past four World Series, Boston was a big underdog that October. The Braves had momentum on their side. Not only did Boston upset the A's, they became the first team to sweep an opponent in four games. James and Rudolph were dominant. Each recorded two wins, and the pair combined to allow one earned run in 29 innings.

Miracle sports teams? The Boston Braves of 1914 were the first.

College Crew

On July 8, Harvard's junior varsity eight became the first U.S. rowing crew to win the prestigious Grand Challenge Cup at the Henley Royal Regatta in England. That was the first of five Grand Challenge Cup championships for the Harvard Crimson. The university's varsity crew also took the Cup in 1939, 1951, 1959, and 1985.

Crew, in fact, remains an important part of the Harvard sporting scene even today. The Crimson have won several national championships in the sport, and the annual Harvard-Yale regatta is the oldest intercollegiate sporting event in the country.

In addition, Harvard oarsmen have competed in every Olympics since 1936.

Sir Walter

Golfer Walter Hagen won the first of his 11 career majors (at the time, golf's four major championships were the U.S. Open, the U.S. Amateur, the British Open, and the British Amateur; today's four majors are the Masters, the U.S. Open, the British Open, and the PGA Championship), capturing the U.S. Open at Midlothian Country Club in Blue Island, Illinois on August 21.

Hagen was only 21 years and playing in just his second U.S. Open when he led after each round en route to the 1914 title at the club just outside of Chicago.

He took command of the tournament with an opening-round 68, and closed the final round strong, too, with a one-under-par 35 for the final nine holes. Still, he had to hold off Chick Evans by one shot. Evans narrowly missed a long putt on the final hole that would have forced a playoff.

Hagen was born in Rochester, New York, but his ancestors were German and Irish. One of golf's most colorful personalities, he lived lavishly, and was one of the first players in the sport to recognize, and to capitalize on, the financial opportunities that being a world-class golfer presented. He also was an excellent all-around athlete who could have signed with baseball's Philadelphia Phillies.

After winning the 1914 U.S. Open, however, he stuck with golf. And eight years later, he became the first American to win the British Open when he took the event at Sandwich, England.

Hagen went on to win the British Open four times in all. He also won five PGA titles and two U.S. Opens.

By the way, Hagen earned $300 for his victory at the 1914 U.S. Open. By contrast, 2003 U.S. Open champion Jim Furyk pocketed more than $1 million for winning that year's tournament at Olympia Fields in Illinois.

A Titanic Tennis Title

When Richard Williams lost to Maurice McLoughlin in the finals of the 1913 U.S. Tennis Championships (now the U.S. Open), he was hardly distraught. Williams had a unique sense of perspective among American sportsmen: A year earlier, he had been a passenger on the ill-fated *Titanic*.

In the spring of 1912, Williams, then 21, was aboard the "greatest ship afloat" with his father, Duane, an attorney. The American family lived in Switzerland and Duane was accompanying Richard to Harvard University, where he was to enroll. Instead, tragedy struck. Just after midnight on April 15, 1912, the *Titanic* struck

1914

an iceberg in the north Atlantic. Duane Williams was killed when one of the mighty ship's funnels fell on top of him. Richard jumped overboard into the calm, but freezing, water. He found a collapsible life raft to cling to, and six hours later was plucked from the water.

Nearly 1,500 of the *Titanic's* 2,201 passengers died. "I do not believe that more than five percent of the people drowned," Williams later said of those who went into the Atlantic with him, "but they froze to death." Williams was lucky to be alive, but a doctor on board the rescue vessel recommended that his legs be amputated. Williams refused, and though his legs were numb, he stood up and began walking around to regain circulation in them. The pain was excruciating. "As I tried to stand, it was like thousands of needles going through my legs," he later recalled.

Williams avoided the surgeon's blade. The following year, 1913, he helped the United States to its first Davis Cup victory in 11 years and lost to McLoughlin in the U.S. Tennis Championships.

This year he returned to the U.S. Championships at Newport, Rhode Island. Again his foe was McLoughlin, the two-time reigning champ. This time, however, Williams overcame McLoughlin. The *Titanic* survivor won in straight sets, 6–3, 8–6, 10–8, in June. Considering where Williams had been in the pre-dawn hours of April 16 two year earlier, has there ever been a greater comeback?

Other Milestones of 1914

✔ On July 11, rookie baseball pitcher George Herman "Babe" Ruth debuted for the Boston Red Sox. Ruth defeated the Cleveland Indians 4–3, although he was taken out for a pinch-hitter in the seventh inning.

✔ For the second consecutive year, New York Giants pitcher Christy Mathewson had more victories (24) than walks allowed (23).

✔ The Yale Bowl, by far the nation's largest football venue with a seating capacity of 60,000, opened on November 21 in New Haven, Conn. Harvard won 36-0. A newspaper account proclaimed: "Yale had the Bowl—but Harvard had the punch."

✔ In Chicago, Weeghman Park, later to be renamed Wrigley Field, opened as the home of the Federal League's Chicago Whales. It eventually became the home of the Chicago Cubs.

✔ Honus Wagner and Napoleon Lajoie become the second and third batters in Major League Baseball history to collect 3,000 career hits (Cap Anson was the first).

The Ladies' Open

Mary K. Browne was born in Ventura, California, in 1881. Like many great athletes, Browne's tale of triumph is a paradox: She was a sickly child and so turned to sports as a way to regain her health. Not only did Browne get better, but in the world of tennis, she got to be the best.

By 1914 Browne was the two-time defending champion at the U.S. Tennis Championships. She defeated Eleanora Sears in straight sets in 1912 and Dorothy Green, also in straight sets, in 1913.

Browne was a superb volleyer and was one of the first women players to rush the net as an offensive strategy, during an era when the baseline ground-strokes game was standard among all tennis players.

In 1914 Browne, now 23 years old, met Mary Wagner in the finals at Newport, Rhode Island on June 13. Wagner provided stiffer competition, extending Browne to a third set. Browne eventually won, though, 6–1, 1–6, 6–1.

The win was Browne's third, and final, U.S. Tennis Championship triumph. Ten years later, she gained more renown for her talents as a two-sport athlete. During a two-week period in the summer of 1924, Browne, a self-taught golfer, competed in the national championships for both tennis and golf. In the U.S. Tennis Championship (now called the U.S. Open), she reached the semifinals, losing to Helen Wills, and in the U.S. Women's Amateur Golf Championship in Nyatt, Rhode Island, she advanced all the way to the finals before succumbing to Dorothy Campbell.

No woman before or since has advanced to the semifinals of the country's most prestigious championships in both tennis and golf.

Twice as Good *Mary K. Browne not only was a dominant tennis player who won three U.S. titles, but she also was a star golfer, too.*

1915

Race and the Ring

Jack Johnson's 6 1/2-year reign as boxing's first African-American heavyweight champion (see pages 52 and 60) came to an end on April 5, in Havana, Cuba, when Jess Willard, a 6-foot-5, 250-pound Kansas farmer, knocked out Johnson in the 26th round of their scheduled 45-round match. The 37-year-old Johnson outboxed Willard, 28, for the first 20 rounds, but the older fighter seemed to punch himself out in the Cuban heat. That's when Willard, at the time the largest man to ever enter a prize ring, flicked a left jab to his opponent's heart and then slammed a right to his jaw, sending the champ to the canvas as referee Jack Welch counted him out at 10.

After the fight, Johnson announced his retirement. He returned to the United States in 1920 and served a 366-day sentence for violating the Mann Act (which at the time made it a crime for him to have traveled with a white woman across state lines) at the federal prison in Leavenworth, Kansas. He died in a car accident in Raleigh, North Carolina, in 1946, the year before Jackie Robinson became the first black baseball player in the major leagues.

Girl Power

On May 8, Regret became the first filly (female horse) to win the Kentucky Derby, which had been run since 1875. Jockey Joe Notter rode the favored 3-year-old to a wire-to-wire victory, holding off a strong stretch drive by Pebbles to finish two lengths in front. The filly's much-anticipated victory gave the annual race in Louisville, Kentucky, a strong dose of national publicity. Colonel Matt Winn, who owned the Churchill Downs track where the race was staged, explained the significance Regret had in Derby history: "The race needed only a victory by Regret to create some more coast-to-coast publicity to really put it over [the top]. She did not fail us. Regret made the Kentucky Derby an American institution." It was 65 years before another filly, Genuine Risk in 1980, would win the prestigious race. In 1988, Winning Colors became the third filly to win the 1 1/2-mile event.

On May 22, the thoroughbred Rhine Maiden, with Douglas Hoffman in the saddle, became the third filly to win the Preakness Stakes when she held off Half Rock by a length and a half and finished in 1:58. Rhine Maiden's victory, coupled

Reign Man *Jess Willard knocked out Jack Johnson to become boxing's new heavyweight champion.*

with Regret's win in the Kentucky Derby, produced the only Kentucky Derby-Preakness Stakes wins by fillies in the same year. (Regret did not compete in the 1915 Preakness.) No filly has won the Preakness since Nellie Morse in 1924.

The Grey Ghost

Race car driver Ralph DePalma, who had a legendary rivalry with Bar-ney Oldfield, drove his Mercedes Grey Ghost at an average speed of 89.840 m.p.h. to win the $22,600 purse at the fifth running of the Indianapolis 500, on May 31. The victory was especially sweet for De-Palma, who had suffered a devastating loss in the 500-mile race in 1912 (see page 69). This time, DePalma led 132 of the 200 laps, including the most important lap of all—the final one. Still, tough luck almost burned him again. DePalma's Mercedes

1915

was running on only three of its six cylinders when it crossed the finish line.

The Big Apple Open

In tennis, the U.S. singles championship was played for the first time at the West Side Tennis Club in Forest Hills, New York. Bill Johnston defeated Maurice McLoughlin in four sets on September 7, a day before Molla Bjurstedt won the first of four straight titles by besting Hazel Hotchkiss Wightman in three sets. The men's and women's titles had been held at Newport Casino in Newport, Rhode Island, since 1881. The move to Forest Hills, located just outside New York City, was made as tennis was gaining in popularity and the West Side facility provided a larger stadium with better access. The West Side Tennis Club hosted the U.S. Open until 1977, when the tournament moved to its current location at Flushing Meadows in Queens, New York.

Flag Day *Three years after bad luck cost him a victory at the Indianapolis 500, driver Ralph DePalma took the checkered flag to win the pretigious race in 1915.*

Baseball in the Courts

The first major battle for the public's sporting dollars was settled on December 22, in Cincinnati, when an agreement was negotiated between the Federal League and Major League Baseball. The battle had lasted nearly two years before the American and National Leagues agreed to forgive those players that had jumped to the rival Federal League, and allowed them to be reinstated and placed in a pool of players made eligible for a special draft. Teams then were allowed to buy back those players, causing a scramble for the best players to sell their services to the highest bidder.

Two Federal League owners were allowed to purchase existing major league teams. Charles Weeghman, who had been owner of the Federal League's 1914 pennant-winning Chicago Whales, took over the Chicago Cubs of the National League. Philip Ball of the St. Louis Terriers took control of the St. Louis Browns of the American League. The conditions of these sales later became clear when the players from the Federal League clubs in Chicago and St. Louis were required to join the respective clubs in the National and American Leagues.

All was not over, however, as the Baltimore franchise refused to drop the Federal League's legal claim against organized baseball as being in violation of anti-trust laws of fair business practices that was currently before Judge Kenesaw Mountain Landis (who eventually would become the game's first commissioner by the end of the decade). Baltimore pursued the lawsuit all the way to the U.S. Supreme Court. The result was a 1922 decision by Justice Oliver Wendell Holmes that gave Major League Baseball the ability to operate without competition. The ruling stands today, and because of it, no rival baseball league has since competed against the American and National Leagues.

In addition, Major League Baseball has enjoyed the protection of the courts in its dealings with member clubs as they tried to move between cities or otherwise change their status.

Other Milestones of 1915

✔ In January, the great Hawaiian swimmer and surfer Duke Kahanamoku, along with other aquatic stars, visited the swimming-obsessed country of Australia. While there, Duke broke his own world record for the 100-yard swim with a time of 53.8 seconds. But it was the fantastic surfing conditions that excited the Duke, and his legendary surfboard riding display at Freshwater Beach near Sydney was the first demonstration of the sport outside the United States. The Hawaiian surfing pioneer had a major impact on surfing in Australia. Today, there are nearly 2.5 million surfers in that country.

✔ On May 6, a young pitcher for the Boston Red Sox named Babe Ruth hit the first of his 714 career home runs. It came against the New York Yankees.

✔ Ty Cobb of the Detroit Tigers hit .369 to lead all American League batters for a record ninth year in a row. He also stole 96 bases, a record that would stand until Maury Wills of the Los Angeles Dodgers swiped 104 bases in 1962.

✔ Al Sharpe coached the Cornell University football squad to a 9-0 record and captured the school's first national championship on the gridiron.

1916

The Rose Bowl Returns

In 1901 the Tournament of Roses Association of Pasadena, California, decided to hold a January 1 football game in conjunction with other New Year's Day festivities. Thus, on the first day of 1902 the University of Michigan met Stanford University in the first college bowl game. The Michigan Wolverines mauled their California counterparts 49–0. The game was ended mercifully with nine minutes remaining. So ugly was the outcome that the committee reverted to other forms of sporting entertainment over the next 13 years. In place of football, there were chariot races and even a race pitting a camel against an elephant.

Finally, in 1915, the Tournament of Roses Committee reconsidered. "We better go back to football," said committee president Lewis Turner, "so we can give newspapermen from coast to coast something to write about."

Washington State (6–0) and Brown University (5–3–1) were selected to play at Tournament Park (the Rose Bowl itself would not be built until 1923) on January 1, 1916. The weeks leading up to the game were unusual, to say the least. First, days

of heavy rain and even snow turned the field into an ocean of mud. Second, Washington State's players were rising at 5 a.m. each day to serve as extras in a football film entitled *Tom Brown of Harvard*. Each player earned $100 for his 14 mornings of work.

The lost sleep did not adversely affect the Washington State Cougars. Brown's star back, Fritz Pollard, the first black All-American, was held to 47 yards on 13 carries. The Cougars scored two second-half touchdowns to win 14–0. The Rose Bowl, also known as "The Granddaddy of Them All," has been played every year since.

First PGA Champ

On January 17, 35 professional golfers, including Walter Hagen, attended a meeting hosted by Rodman Wanamaker, a department store magnate and sports enthusiast. Two years earlier Wanamaker had created the Millrose Games. To this day that track meet, held annually in New York City, draws some of the world's greatest athletes.

On this day, Wanamaker proposed the idea for a national championship of golf. Thus was the Professional Golfers

Before Pinstripes *Babe Ruth made his mark pitching in Boston before becoming a slugger in New York. He helped the Red Sox win the World Series in 1916 (see page 90).*

Association Championship born, with Wanamaker chipping in a trophy and a cash prize of $2,580 for the match play event. In match play, a point is earned for each hole won, rather than stroke play, which counts the total number of strokes for all 18 holes.

On October 10, 16 golfers assembled at the Siwanoy Country Club in Bronxville, New York. The finals pitted "Long Jim" Barnes of England against Jock Hutchison of Scotland. Barnes won on the final hole, and his name is the first engraved on the Wanamaker Trophy as PGA champion.

1916

222–0

On October 7, Georgia Institute of Technology defeated Cumberland University in the greatest mismatch in college football history. If the score, 222–0, fails to convey Georgia Tech's utter dominance of the contest, consider this: Neither team had a first down. Cumberland was too inept and Tech, coached by John Heisman, scored every time that its offense ran a play from scrimmage.

For Heisman (who now is much better known for the trophy that is given in his name to the best college football player of the year), the game was a kind of revenge. The previous spring, Cumberland's baseball team had spanked Tech, 22–0.

Cumberland discontinued football in 1916. However, it had earlier agreed to play Tech and honored the deal. The Lebanon, Tennessee, school sent 15 ill-prepared players to Atlanta for the game, and they were utterly outplayed. Their total offensive output was minus 28 yards. How bad was it? Late in the game a Cumberland fumble rolled toward Cumberland's B.F. Paty. "Pick it up!" the fumbler shouted to Paty. "Pick it up yourself," Paty replied. "You dropped it."

The game, mercifully, was halted with 15 minutes remaining.

Red Sox Win World Series—Again

The Boston Red Sox won their third American League pennant in five seasons and second in a row in 1916. Their opponent was the Brooklyn

Baseball Records

A number of outstanding and peculiar Major League Baseball records were set in 1916. Among them:

The New York Giants won 26 consecutive games in September. Despite that streak and an earlier 17-game string, the Giants finished in fourth place in the National League with an 86–66 record. During their 26-game run, the Giants were helped twice by Mother Nature. Trailing the Cincinnati Reds 2–0 in the fourth inning on September 15, New York was saved when the game was called on account of rain. Three days later, the score was tied 1–1 in the eighth inning of the second game of a doubleheader with the Pittsburgh Pirates when the game was called due to darkness.

The Philadelphia Athletics, winners of three of the decade's six World Series so far under manager Connie Mack, lost 20 consecutive games and finishes in last place (36–117) in the American League. Following a July 21 home loss at Shibe Park, the A's lost a major league-record 19 straight road games.

On September 24, Marty Kavanagh of the Cleveland Indians belted the first pinch-hit grand slam in American League history. Kavanagh's game-winning home run off the Boston Red Sox's Dutch Leonard rolled through a hole in the fence at League Park and could not be retrieved before Kavanagh rounded the bases in Cleveland's 5–3 victory.

Other Milestones of 1916

✔ World War I had broken out in Europe, and the Olympics, which had been staged every four years since 1896, were canceled. They had been scheduled to be held in Berlin, Germany that summer.

✔ Although the formation of the National Hockey League was still two years away, the Montreal Canadiens won their first Stanley Cup, three games to two, over the Portland Rosebuds, on March 30.

✔ On June 26, baseball's Cleveland Indians, in a 2–0 win against the Chicago White Sox, wore numbers pinned to their sleeves, thus becoming the first baseball team to have uniform numbers. At that time, a player's number corresponded to his position in the batting order—so the number could change as the batting order changed.

Chick Evans

✔ Chicago Cubs owner Charles Weeghman introduced a baseball innovation that remains popular today: Fans were allowed to keep baseballs that are hit into the stands.

✔ Using only seven hickory-shaft clubs, Chick Evans became the first golfer to win the United States Amateur and the United States Open in the same year.

✔ The NCAA and the Amateur Athletic Union (A.A.U.) formed the Joint Basketball Rules Committee to standardize the rules of basketball across the nation.

✔ Forty women competed in the first Women's National Bowling Association Tournament (now the Women's International Bowling Congress Championship Tournament) on November 27 and 28 at Washington Bowling Alleys and Billiard Parlors in St. Louis. Agnes Koester of Detroit was the winner.

Dodgers, who were then better-known as the Robins.

Boston won game one of the October Series at home 6–5. Game two, also in Boston, was a pitchers' duel between Brooklyn's Sherry Smith and Boston left-hander Babe Ruth. Before he was a slugger, Ruth was a terrific pitcher. In 1916, only his second full season in the majors, the 21-year-old won 23 games and led the A.L. with a 1.75 ERA. He did not allow a home run during the season.

Brooklyn's leadoff hitter in game two, center fielder Hy Myers, put a blemish on Ruth's homer-less streak. Myers hit a line drive to right field that skipped under the glove of Boston's Harry Hooper. Myers scored on the inside-the-park home run. Ruth evened the score himself two innings later, hitting into a ground-out that scored a run.

For the next 10 innings, neither team scored a run off Smith or Ruth. Finally, in the bottom of the 14th inning Red Sox pinch-hitter Del Gainor singled in Mike McNally from second base for the 2–1 victory. Ruth, after allowing the leadoff homer, had pitched 14 innings of shutout ball (he later extended that mark to a Series-record 29 2/3 innings).

The Red Sox, up 2–0 in the Series, eventually won four games to one.

1917

United States Enters World War I

On April 6, the United States Senate and House of Representatives voted overwhelmingly to declare war on Germany. The United States had formally entered a war that was sparked in 1914 after Archduke Franz Ferdinand, heir to the throne of the Austro-Hungarian Empire, was assassinated in Sarajevo, then a part of Russia. When Austria-Hungary declared war on Russia, Germany joined in against Russia, igniting a skirmish that spread among European and Asian countries. The United States joined on the side of Great Britain, France, Russia, Belgium, Italy, Japan, and other allies to defeat Germany, Austria-Hungary, Turkey, and Bulgaria. The entrance of the U.S. into this battle made it the first World War, also called The Great War.

The war exacted a toll on every aspect of American life, including sports. In 1917 a number of major sporting events were canceled, and athletes decided whether or not to enlist with the armed forces. The annual Indianapolis 500 auto race was canceled. In golf the U.S. Open and the PGA Championship were canceled. All boxing titles were frozen during the next two years.

College football, if not the first casualty of the war, certainly suffered the most in 1917. No All-Americans were selected. Some major college football programs, among them the University of Georgia, University of North Carolina, and University of Tennessee, did not field teams. The Rose Bowl that capped the college season on January 1, 1918, resembled a military engagement as the Mare Island Marines defeated Camp Lewis Army, 19–7.

Exactly seven months earlier, many Americans realized that sports would not be immune to the war. On June 1, Boston Braves catcher Hank Gowdy, a hero of the 1914 World Series, enlisted with the Ohio National Guard. He became the first Major League Baseball player to enlist in the armed forces.

Ernie Shore's Perfect Game

One of the strangest perfect games in baseball—no hits, no walks, no errors, no hit batsmen, just 27 batters up, 27 down—began with Babe Ruth. On June 23 Ruth took the mound for the Boston

What a Relief! *Boston's Ernie Shore (right) was perfect after taking over for Babe Ruth (left) against Washington.*

Red Sox in the first game of a double-header against the Washington Senators at Boston's Fenway Park. Ruth must have been in an irritable mood that afternoon. His first pitch to Senator leadoff batter Ray Morgan was called a ball. Ruth did not like the call, and left the mound to argue with umpire Brick Owens. His second and third pitches were also called balls, and after each one Ruth barked at Owens.

Ruth's fourth pitch was called ball four. Ruth went berserk. He approached home plate and socked Owens in the jaw. For that, Ruth was ejected from the game (and was suspended for nine days and fined $100).

1917

Enter Red Sox teammate Ernie Shore. A starting pitcher who had won one game in each of the previous two World Series for Boston, Shore picked Morgan off first base. One out. From there Shore was simply perfect. He faced 26 Washington batters and retired each one of them, as the Red Sox won 4–0.

Was it a perfect game? For years baseball said it was, since Shore entered the game before one out had been recorded. Finally, in 1990 baseball reversed the judgment on Shore's "perfect game." The new rule said that for a pitcher to pitch a perfect game, he must start and finish it.

Giants Lose World Series—Again

No baseball team provided more heartbreak during the decade than the New York Giants. Manager John McGraw had taken the team to the World Series in 1911, 1912, and 1913 and lost all three times. In 1917, the outcome was the same. The Giants lost the World Series that October in six games to the Chicago White Sox. Pitcher Red Faber, a spitballer, was the White Sox star, winning games one, five (he pitched two innings of relief), and six.

Game six was another tale of heartbreak for Giant fans. With no score in the fourth inning at New York's Polo Grounds, Chicago's Eddie Collins reached on an error. The next batter, "Shoeless" Joe Jackson, hit a pop-up that Giant rightfielder Dave Robertson dropped. Runners on first and third, no outs.

Happy Felsch then grounded back to the Giants pitcher, Rube Benton, who noticed that Collins had strayed too far off third base. Benton tossed the ball to Zimmerman, the third baseman. Collins sprinted home, past catcher Bill Rariden who had carelessly walked away from home plate. Zimmerman raced Collins home. Collins slid safely before Zimmerman could tag him.

The White Sox won this game, and the Series, 4–2.

Other Milestones of 1917

✔ On March 26 the Seattle Metropolitans of the Pacific Coast Hockey Association became the first U.S.-based team to win the Stanley Cup. The Metropolitans beat the Montreal Canadiens, three games to one.

✔ On May 2 at Chicago's Weeghman Park, 3,500 fans witnessed baseball's first double nine-inning no-hitter. Righthander Fred Toney pitched for the visiting Cincinnati Reds while James "Hippo" Vaughn, a southpaw, was on the mound for the Cubs. Neither pitcher surrendered a hit through nine innings. The Reds won in the 10th inning as Jim Thorpe—yes, that Jim Thorpe—got the game-winning hit on a swinging bunt. Toney retired the Cubs in order in the bottom of the 10th to preserve his no-hitter.

✔ On August 17, Gertrude Ederle, a 12-year-old swimmer, zipped through the women's 880-yard freestyle event in 13 minutes, 19 seconds at a meet in Indianapolis, Indiana, becoming the youngest person ever to set a world record. Nine years later, she attempted to swim the English Channel.

✔ Henry Hall ski jumped a U.S.-record 203 feet at Steamboat Springs, Colorado. Hall was the first to jump over 200 feet, breaking the previous mark by 11 feet.

Benny Leonard

Benny Leonard literally fell into his profession. Growing up the son of Orthodox Jewish parents on Manhattan's Lower East Side, young Benjamin Leiner loved boxing. In September of 1911, when he was 15, Benjamin went to watch the fights at a local club. The only problem was that he was too poor to buy a ticket. So Leiner climbed to a skylight above the club and peered down into the ring. He lost his balance and fell through the window, right into the ring, to the surprise and anger of the club's owners.

Unable to pay for the damage he had caused, Leiner promised to take the place of a fighter who had failed to appear that night. He lost, but a career and a ring name—Benny Leonard—were born.

Six years later Leonard, then only 21, fought Freddie Welsh for the lightweight title. On May 28 Welsh, the champ, and Leonard met in New York City.

Welsh and Leonard had fought twice previously, but both bouts ended in no decisions. On this night Leonard dominated the champion. In the ninth round Leonard knocked Welsh out cold.

Leonard retained the world lightweight title for 7 1/2 years. He retired with a career record of 86–5–1. Today he is still considered perhaps the greatest lightweight in boxing history.

Good Career Move *Benny Leonard, who literally fell into his profession as a boxer, went on to become one of the greatest lightweight champions in history.*

The NHL Is Born

On November 26 a meeting took place inside Montreal's Windsor Hotel. Earlier in the year the National Hockey Association had decided to reorganize. Representatives from five of those teams—the Ottawa Senators, Montreal Wanderers, Montreal Canadiens, Toronto Arenas, and Quebec Bulldogs—met to form a new hockey league. They called it the National Hockey League (NHL).

Before the season even began, the Quebec Bulldogs opted not to field a team. Too many Bulldogs skaters had joined the armed forces.

Finally, on December 19, the NHL opened play with a pair of games in Montreal played in front of 700 fans.

1918

Over There!

🏆 By 1918 the effects of World War I could be felt throughout American life, from the institution of Daylight Savings Time (so there were more hours of daylight for war production work) to the cancellation of many sporting events.

College football continued to be hardest hit. More military football squads sprouted up in 1917 and 1918 as many college football teams were discontinued. More than 20 schools eliminated football this year, among them former national champions Cornell University and Yale, as well as future champs University of Alabama, Louisiana State University, and University of Washington. Notre Dame, on the other hand, named Knute Rockne coach and athletic director in February.

In July, Major League Baseball voted to shorten its season from 154 games to 125. The regular season ended a month early, on September 2. The World Series was allowed to be staged, ruled Secretary of War Newton D. Baker, as long as 10 percent of its revenues were given to war charities. The players received all-time lows in winner's and loser's shares. The winner's share was $1,102 per man.

The most famous athletes, such as boxer Jack Dempsey and slugger Babe Ruth, were not called to war. They were allowed to continue entertaining American citizens who were working hard at home to support the war effort overseas. Other patriotic athletes, such as pitcher Christy Mathewson and Indy 500 racer Edward Rickenbacker, decided to enlist in the armed forces anyway, and they became World War I heroes. Rickenbacker earned far more fame as the United States' top flying ace than he ever had in four races at Indy. The "American Ace of Aces," as Rickenbacker was known, shot down 22 enemy aircraft and four reconnaissance balloons over the skies of Europe.

Others were not so lucky. Mathewson trained as an officer in the Chemical Corps, working to defend U.S. troops from dangerous gases used by enemy forces in the trenches of Europe. During training, Mathewson inhaled some of the gases and his lungs were permanently scarred. The illness caused by the gassing would eventually take his life in 1925 at the age of only 45. Hobey Baker, who had been captain of Princeton University's football and hockey teams earlier in the decade, and who flew with Rickenbacker's

War Hero *Race car driver Edward Rickenbacker also earned considerable acclaim as a World War I flying ace.*

squadron, was killed while test-piloting an aircraft in France. His name lives on today—the nation's top college hockey player is given the Hobey Baker Award.

Some athletes went to war. Some stayed home. Others did both. Future baseball Hall of Famer Rabbit Maranville joined the Navy. Then in July he was granted a 10-day leave. The infielder headed straight to his old team, the Boston Braves. Maranville batted .316 in 11 games before returning to sea.

Red Sox Beat Cubs in World Series

Both the Boston Red Sox and the Chicago Cubs made their fifth World Series appearance in 1918. Boston, which had won all four World Series in which it had played, was Major League Baseball's most successful postseason franchise.

Because of the abbreviated regular season, this Fall Classic took place in late summer, from September 5 to 11. To re-

1918

duce train use (another war consideration), the first three games were played in Chicago and then the Series moved to Boston.

Babe Ruth, who won 13 games during the regular season, outdueled the Cubs' 22-game winner, Hippo Vaughn, in Game 1, 1–0. Ruth's complete-game shutout, added to his 13 scoreless innings in the 1916 World Series, gave him 22 consecutive scoreless innings pitched in the Series. By the end of this Series, his record had reached 29 straight, a mark that would stand for more than 40 years.

Another highlight of the opener: During the seventh-inning stretch a military band played "The Star-Spangled Banner," which was not yet the National Anthem (that did not happen until 1931). From then on the song has been played at every World Series game.

Lefty Tyler, a 19-game winner during the regular season, won game two for Chicago 2–1, but Boston regained the Series lead when Carl Mays beat Vaughn 2–1 in the next game.

Vaughn won Game 5, but Mays' three-hitter in Boston's 2–1 victory in Game 6 ended it.

The Series was a defensive gem. The Red Sox batted just .186, the all-time low for a World Series winner (the Cubs hit .210), but only committed one error (also a record for a six-game World Series). No team ever scored more than three runs in one game. No home runs were hit.

The 1918 World Series, however, has gained immortality for an entirely different reason. Why? Because neither of its contestants, the Cubs or the Red Sox, have won a World Series since.

Toronto Arenas Are First NHL Champs

The first National Hockey League season began on December 19, 1917, with four teams: the Montreal Canadiens, Montreal Wanderers, Ottawa Senators and Toronto Arenas. Two weeks later, only three teams remained.

On January 3, Montreal's Westmount Arena, the home ice of both the Canadiens and the Wanderers, was destroyed by a fire. The Canadiens moved to the smaller Jubilee Ice Rink. The Wanderers, who from the outset had complained about a shortage of skaters due to World War I, chose to cancel their season.

The infant hockey league played on. The format was for a 22-game season to be played in two halves. The winner of the first half would play the winner of the second half for the NHL title. The winner would advance to play the Pacific Coast Hockey Association (PCHA) champ for the Stanley Cup.

Montreal defeated Toronto 10–9 in the first NHL game ever played. The Canadiens went on to win the season's first half. A week later, Arenas manager Charlie Querrie went missing. Querrie decided to "disappear" for 10 days because he felt that his authority was being usurped by management.

On January 5 Querrie returned, and luck started gliding in Toronto's favor. It had been forbidden for goaltenders to fall onto the ice while making a save (they were fined $2 per infraction), but the NHL eliminated the rule in January. Also, after the Wanderers disbanded, Querrie signed their goalie, Harry Holmes.

Toronto won the second half of the season, then outlasted the Canadiens during the two-game playoff, 10 goals to 7. The Arenas met the Vancouver Millionaires and their high-scoring forward, Cyclone Taylor, in a best-of-five series for the Stanley Cup in March. After splitting the first four games, Toronto won the clincher, 2–1. For the first time, an NHL team won the Stanley Cup. More importantly, the new league survived a tumultuous first season.

Magical Molla Bjurstedt

Molla Bjurstedt was a tennis legend in her native Norway by the age of 21. Bjurstedt won eight Norwegian national championships. In 1914 she sailed to New York to visit relatives. She liked it there so much that she decided to stay.

A year later, Bjurstedt attended the men's national indoor tournament in New York as a spectator. But when she learned there was a women's competition, she entered—and won.

For the next four years Bjurstedt dominated tennis in her adopted country. She won the U.S. Open on the grass courts of the Philadelphia Cricket Club four straight years, from 1915 to 1918. Her final victory in the streak, on June 22, came at the expense of Eleanor Goss, 6–4, 6–3.

Also in 1918, Bjurstedt won her third U.S. indoor singles title in September. The following year Bjurstedt married American Franklin Mallory. As Molla Bjurstedt Mallory she won four more U.S. Open singles titles, the last at age 42 in 1926 (still the oldest women's major champion). Her eight singles crowns at the Open remains the women's record.

Other Milestones of 1918

✔ On May 14, lawmakers in Washington, D.C. made it legal to play baseball on Sundays. The populations of major cities were increasing with soldiers returning from the war, and lawmakers wanted to provide these working people with recreation and amusement.

✔ African-American end Paul Robeson of Rutgers University, the son of a slave, was named an All-American and graduated as the school's valedictorian. Robeson later went on to become a

Paul Robeson

lawyer, acclaimed actor, singer, and civil rights activist.

✔ Heavyweight boxing contender Jack Dempsey won 15 of 16 bouts in 1918 and avenged a 1917 knockout by "Fireman" Jim Flynn (the only knockout in Dempsey's entire career) with a Valentine's Day first-round knockout of Flynn. Dempsey's other first-round victims included Fred Fulton (after only 18 seconds of fighting) and Carl Morris (after 14 seconds).

1919

The Black Sox Scandal

World War I ended in November of 1918. Major League Baseball, sensing increasing postwar interest in the national pastime, chose to make the World Series a best-of-nine affair. The Series would be remembered, though, as the darkest moment in baseball.

The Chicago White Sox were appearing in the World Series for the second time in three years (they beat the New York Giants in six games in 1917). They were the heavy favorites against the Cincinnati Reds, even though the Reds had won 96 of 140 games during the regular season while crusing to the National League pennant; the White Sox won 88 times en route to the A.L. crown.

The White Sox players, however, hated their owner, Charles Comiskey, because they felt he did not pay them their due; in fact, they were paid less than players on other teams. He was also legendarily cheap: Chicago's uniforms were often filthy because of Comiskey's order to cut down the laundry bill. In 1917 Comiskey promised the club a bonus for winning the pennant. All they got was a case of cheap Champagne.

Tiring of Comiskey's penny-pinching, eight players decided to accept money from gamblers to "fix" (purposely lose) the World Series. Competing at less than full strength, the Sox played uninspired baseball. In the bottom of the first inning of game one, Chicago's 29-game winner, Eddie Cicotte, hit Red leadoff hitter Morrie Rath with a pitch. Supposedly, Cicotte's pitch was more than an errant toss. It was a signal to bettors that a few members of the White Sox

Scandalous *Several members of the A.L.-champion Chicago White Sox gave baseball its biggest black eye in 1919.*

planned to "fix" the Series—lose on purpose, so the gamblers could boost their winnings.

The Sox lost game one, 9–1, and game two, 4–2. After the second loss, Chicago manager Kid Gleason confided to Comiskey, that he was suspicious of his players. Baseball's three-man National Commission was told of those fears, but did not take action. Newspaper reporters,

such as Ring Lardner, also suspected something was awry after the Sox, who won game three, were shut out in games four and five.

Chicago fell behind 4–0 in game six with the "help" of two errors by shortstop Swede Risberg and one error by centerfielder Happy Felsch. The Sox, rallied, however, to win 5–4 in 10 innings. In game seven Cicotte, who had already lost two

1919

games and committed two errors, pitched a seven-hitter as the Sox won, 4–1.

The Reds, however, clinched the Series in game 8. Cincinnati scored four first-inning runs off Chicago's Lefty Williams and ran away with a 10–5 win. The loss was Williams' third in the Series (his ERA was 6.61), which seemed odd for a pitcher who had gone 23–11 during the season.

During the Series, and especially after, rumors swirled that a few of the Sox had been taken money in exchange for not playing their best, so that bettors could be assured the underdog Reds would win. Baseball team owners and league officials were concerned. Even the slightest hint of gamblers' involvement would spoil baseball's honest image. The owners grew so worried that fans would lose faith in the game's integrity that they hired a federal judge named Kenesaw Mountain Landis to become baseball's first commissioner.

The following year, eight White Sox confessed to their role in what became known as the "Black Sox Scandal." Though cleared in a court of law of any wrongdoing—the players were promised between $5,000 to $10,000 by some local gamblers to throw the Series, but never collected all of the money—it made no difference to Judge Landis. He banned all eight players from baseball for life. They were pitchers Cicotte and Williams, centerfielder Felsch, shortstop Risberg, first baseman Chick Gandil, third baseman Buck Weaver, reserve infielder Fred McMullin, and left-fielder Joe Jackson. "Shoeless Joe," as Jackson was known, actually led all batters in the Series with a .375 average. Because

of his involvement in the scandal, Jackson, whose .356 career batting average is third-best in baseball history, is not in the Baseball Hall of Fame.

No Stanley Cup

Although the NHL began in 1917, the Stanley Cup has been awarded annually since 1893. The lone exception was in 1919, when nobody won the Cup.

Two teams were poised to claim it. The Seattle Metropolitans were champions of the Pacific Coast Hockey Association, and the Montreal Canadiens represented the NHL. After five games in March the series was deadlocked. Each side had two wins; a fifth game was a tie.

However, the Stanley Cup was being played in the midst of a worldwide influenza epidemic. A vaccine did not yet exist for influenza. Approximately 548,000 Americans died, and it was estimated that the contagious disease killed 20 million people worldwide.

During the series a few members of the Canadiens fell ill. The series was postponed, but in the interim Montreal defenseman Bad Joe Hall died from the flu. The Stanley Cup finals were canceled. In hockey tradition, each season, the names of the players from the winning team are engraved on the Cup. That is why no names are engraved on the cup for 1919.

The Dempsey-Willard Fight

Jess Willard was a heavyweight boxing champion who did not like to fight. In 1915, Willard tamed Jack Johnson

New Champion *Jack Dempsey (white trunks) withstood this assault from Jess Willard and won their title bout.*

in the 26th round of their bout in Havana, Cuba, to claim the heavyweight title. In the four years since, Willard, a 6-foot-six Oklahoman who towered over all of his foes, only defended his title once. For Willard, it was good timing. As is stated above, due to the fighting in World War I, all boxing titles were frozen in 1917 and 1918. And in that bout against Frank Moran in 1916, it was stipulated that Willard could only lose his title if he were knocked out. Willard won by decision in 10 rounds.

"I never liked it," Willard once said about boxing. "In fact, I hated it as I never hated a thing previously, but there was money in it."

On July 4, there was $100,000 in it for the champion. The challenger was a young 6-foot-1 upstart named Jack Dempsey. The fight, held at an outdoor arena in 100-degree temperatures in Toledo, Ohio, drew 600 sportswriters. Willard, who had once killed a man in the ring, had little concern for Dempsey.

"There isn't a man living who can hurt me," Willard told a sportswriter before the fight, "no matter where he hits me or how often he lands [punches]."

It took less than one round for Willard to eat those words. In the opening round, after allowing Willard to initiate the action and lulling the champ into a false sense of security, Dempsey attacked with rage. Dempsey knocked Willard to the canvas seven times. At that time a fighter did not have to retreat to a neutral corner after a knockdown, so Dempsey simply hovered over Willard until he began to rise, then hit him again.

Other Milestones of 1919

✔ At the Rose Bowl in Pasadena, California, on New Years Day, Great Lakes Naval Station defeated Mare Island, 17–0.

✔ Howdy Wilcox, an Indianapolis native who raced in every Indianapolis 500 since its 1911 debut, finally won on May 30 in his Peugeot race car.

Sir Barton

✔ Jockey Johnny Loftus rode Sir Barton, a 3-year-old chestnut colt, to a five-length victory over Sweep On at the Belmont Stakes on June 11. Sir Barton became the first colt to win the Kentucky Derby, Preakness States, and the Belmont in the same year. Sir Barton is considered the first Triple Crown winner. However, the phrase "Triple Crown" wasn't coined until 1930, when *Daily Racing Form* writer Charles Hatton used it after Gallant Fox won the three races.

✔ Golfer Walter Hagen won the U.S. Open in an 18-hole playoff by one stroke over Mike Brady at Brae Burn Country Club in West Newton, Mass.

✔ On September 4, Bill Johnston took advantage of young Bill Tilden's weak backhand and won the men's singles final of the U.S. tennis championships at Forest Hills, New York, in straight sets. For Tilden, 26, it was his first time reaching the national final, which he would win the next six years in a row.

✔ In baseball, Red Sox slugger Babe Ruth broke the single-season home run record, with 29. Ty Cobb won his 12th, and last, American League batting title.

The damage? Dempsey knocked out four of Willard's teeth and broke his jaw and cheekbone, as well as three ribs. Willard permanently lost the hearing in his left ear.

Remarkably, Willard answered the bell for rounds two and three (costing the challenger $8,000, as Dempsey had placed a side bet on himself at 10–1 odds for a first round knockout of Willard). After round three, Willard slumped on his stool in a stupor, a victim of the intense heat and Dempsey's intense punches.

The fight was over. Dempsey, who, along with Babe Ruth and football's Red Grange, would be one of the commanding sports figures of the next decade, had just entered his prime.

Man O' War Upset by Upset

How charismatic a thoroughbred horse was Man o' War? This was the first year a horse won the Triple Crown, and Man O' War overshadowed even that three-year old, whose name was Sir Barton.

There are a few reasons for this. First, the Triple Crown (the name for the trio of spring horse races—the Kentucky Derby, Preakness Stakes, and Belmont Stakes) was not known as such until more than a decade later, so winning all three seemed less important. Second, Man o' War was the type of horse you just could not take yours eyes from. Nicknamed "Big Red," although he actually was chestnut-colored, Man o' War was huge, both in height and girth. He ate 12 quarts of oats a day, about one-third more than the average racehorse. His stride, at 28 feet was legendary. And he was spirited.

The first time jockey Johnny Loftus—who also rode Sir Barton to his Triple Crown wins—attempted to mount Man o' War, the horse reportedly tossed him 40 feet. According to his owner, Samuel Riddle, "Tossing Johnny was the last bad move Man o' War ever made."

Make that next-to-last. Man o' War easily won his debut race on June 6 by six lengths. During the summer, the two-year-old won his next five starts, sometimes carrying an impost (the weight a horse must carry in a handicap race) of as much as 130 pounds. Then on August 13, Man o' War was entered in the six-furlong Sanford Memorial Stakes at Saratoga, New York. This was in the era before starting gates, when a tape barrier held the horses back. On this day a substitute starter was in charge of the tape. Man o' War, with Loftus in the saddle, was milling around, his hindquarters facing the tape, when the race began.

Despite that handicap, and despite Loftus making a judgment error in which Man o' War was boxed in against the rail, the horse roared back. He passed every horse in the field, including his chief rival, Golden Broom. Only one horse remained ahead of him—Upset.

But it was too late. Upset broke the tape a neck ahead of Man o' War (contrary to popular belief, this is not how the term "upset" entered the sports lexicon; it was just an incredible coincidence), though in losing Man o' War gained even more admirers. "Though defeated," wrote Fred Van Ness in *The New York Times*, "Man o' War was not discredited."

It was Man o' War's only loss in 10 races this year. It would be the only loss of his magnificent career. To this day, many say that Man o' War was the best thoroughbred who ever ran.

RESOURCES

1900–1919 Events and Personalities

American Decades: 1900-1909
American Decades: 1910-1919
By Vincent Tompkins (Farmington Hills, Mich.: Gale Group, 1996)
This series documents America's history by topic (such as business, science, and sports) and includes essays, timelines, brief biographies, and more.

Coubertin's Olympics: How the Games Began
By Davida Kristy. (Minneapolis: Lucent Books, 1995)
The story behind Baron Pierre de Coubertin's inspiration to re-create the ancient tradition of the Olympic Games.

Jack Johnson: In the Ring and Out
By Jack Johnson (New York: Ameron Ltd., 1993)
A unique autobiography by one of American sports' most important early athletes, this book gives Johnson's own view about his remarkable career. It was first published in 1927.

Major Taylor: The Extraordinary Career of a Champion Rider
By Andrew Ritchie (Baltimore: Johns Hopkins Univ. Press, 1996)
A close-up look at the champion cyclist who broke records and barriers in the first decade of the 20th century.

Jim Thorpe: 20th-Century Jock
By Robert Lipsyte (New York: Harper-Collins, 1993)
An award-winning author tells the story of the man many consider the greatest all-around athlete in American history.

American Sports History

The Complete Book of the Olympics
By David Wallechinsky (New York: Viking Penguin, 2000)
An extremely detailed look at every Winter and Summer Olympics from 1896 to the present, including complete lists of medal winners and short biographies of important American and international athletes.

The Encyclopedia of North American Sports History
By Ralph Hickok (New York: Facts On File, 1992)
This title includes articles on the origins of all the major sports as well as capsule biographies of key figures.

Encyclopedia of World Sport
Edited by David Levinson and Karen Christensen (New York: Oxford University Press, 1999)
This wide-ranging book contains short articles on an enormous variety of sports, personalities, events, and issues, most of which have some connection to American sports history. This is a great starting point for additional research.

ESPN SportsCentury
Edited by Michael McCambridge (New York: Hyperion, 1999)
Created to commemorate the 20th century in sports, this book features essays by well-known sportswriters as well as commentary by popular ESPN broadcasters. Each decade's chapter features an in-depth story about the key event of that time period.

Facts and Dates of American Sports

By Gordon Carruth and Eugene Ehrlich (New York: Harper & Row, 1988)
Very detailed look at sports history, focusing on when events occurred. Large list of birth and death dates for major figures.

An Illustrated History of Boxing

By Nat Fleischer, Sam Andre, Nigel Collins, and Dan Raphael (Secaucus, N.J.: Citadel Press, 6th Edition, 2002)
This book takes you up to the current era of boxing, but it's also an excellent resource for information on some of the sport's earlier stars.

The Sporting News Chronicle of 20th Century Sports

By Ron Smith (New York: BDD/Mallard Press, 1992)
A good single-volume history of key sports events. They are presented as if written right after the event, thus giving the text a "you are there" feel.

Sports of the Times

By David Fischer and William Taafe (New York: Times Books, 2003)
A unique format tracks the top sports events on each day of the calendar year. Find out the biggest event for every day from January 1 to December 31.

Total Baseball

Edited by John Thorn, Pete Palmer, and Michael Gershman (New York: Total Sports, 2004, eighth edition)
The indispensable bible of baseball, it contains the career records of every Major Leaguer. Essays in the front of the book cover baseball history, team history, overviews of baseball in other countries, and articles about the role of women and minorities in the game.

Sports History Web Sites

Hickok Sports

www.hickoksports.com
Not the most beautiful site and devoid of pictures, but filled with a wealth of information on sports at all levels. It is run by Ralph Hickok, an experienced sportswriter, and is regularly updated with the latest winners.

International Boxing Hall of Fame

www.ibhof.com
Legends, lore, enshrinees, and history of the sport that once riveted the American public.

Official Major League Baseball Web Site

www.mlb.com
Each of the major sports leagues has history sections on their official Web sites, but only Major League Baseball's covers the time period in this book.

Official Olympics Web Site

http://www.olympic.org/uk/games/index_uk.asp
Complete history of the Olympic Games, presented by the International Olympic Committee.

The Sporting News "Vault"

www.sportingnews.com/archives
More than 100 years old, The St. Louis-based Sporting News *is the nation's oldest sports weekly. In the history section of its Web site, it has gathered hundreds of articles on sports events, championships, stars, and more. It also includes audio clips of interviews with top names in sports from yesterday and today.*

INDEX